CHINA

W9-CIR-673

CHINA

BY JAMES I. CLARK

McDOUGAL, LITTELL & COMPANY

EVANSTON, ILLINOIS

JAMES I. CLARK, the author of the *Peoples and Cultures Series,* received his B.A. and M.A. in History and his Ph.D. in Education from the University of Wisconsin at Madison. He has taught social studies in elementary and high schools in Wyoming and Wisconsin, and has been an elementary and high school principal. He has also taught at Edgewood College, Madison, Wisconsin, and at the University of Wisconsin at Eau Claire. In addition, he has served as the director of social studies for two major publishing companies. He is author of over a dozen texts on world cultures and American history.

HERMAN OOMS, Associate Professor of History at the University of Illinois, Chicago Circle, is consultant for *China*.

DONALD H. LINDSTROM, Social Studies Coordinator for the West Aurora Schools, Illinois, is consultant for the *Peoples and Cultures Series*.

Editor: Monique de Varennes

Design: William A. Seabright,   Pamela Kimball

Acknowledgments: See page 144

ISBN: 0–88343–628–0

CONTENTS

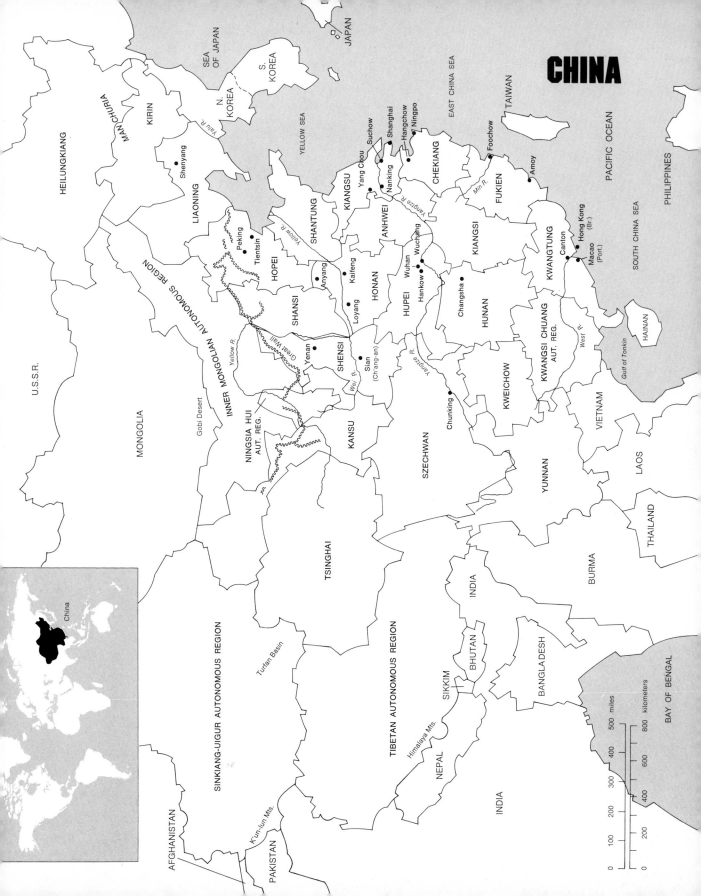

AN ANCIENT CIVILIZATION

Great rivers spawned and nourished civilizations. The Nile in Egypt. The Tigris-Euphrates in Mesopotamia. The Indus in India. The Yellow in China. The Yellow River rises in the K'un-lun Mountains in the west and courses a twisting path eastward to the sea. This tremendous river gave birth to the most enduring civilization the world has ever known.

The Yellow River valley was the home of people during Stone Age times. Peking man, some of whose bones were found in the 1920s near Peking, the capital of China, roamed northern China anywhere from a half million to a million years ago. Tools Peking man and other Stone Age people used were unearthed in the 1960s.

Legend pushes Chinese beginnings far, far back in time. After Earth separated from Heaven, tradition says, the Twelve Emperors of Heaven ruled the universe. Then for a total of 46,500 years the Nine Emperors of Mankind governed the land. Sixteen more emperors followed. Next came the Three Sovereigns, Fu Shi, Shen Nung, and Huang Ti. Under Huang Ti and three later emperors, the people became civilized. They were taught arts and crafts, how to grow crops, and rules of proper conduct. Finally there was Yu, who in about 2000 B.C. began the Hsia Dynasty. This dynasty, under seventeen rulers, endured about five hundred years.

Legend aside, Chinese civilization, which began in the Yellow River valley, is very old. It has been continuous to the present day. And the contributions the Chinese people have made to mankind have been immense.

Opposite: Landscape painted on a hanging scroll by Kung Hsien in the seventeenth century.

THE VALLEY OF THE YELLOW RIVER

The Yellow River is one of several streams flowing north and eastward out of the snow-capped mountains of Central Asia. Most of the rivers die in Inner Mongolia and other semi-desert regions. Only the mighty Yellow breaks through, freeing itself at last from mountains, hills, and deserts, moving out onto a broad floodplain on its way to the sea.

Over the centuries, yellowish-brown soil called loess blowing out of the Gobi Desert built up in the Yellow River valley. In this region where practically no forests grew, winds plastered loess on hills as well as on level stretches. And in Stone Age times, digging into those hills, people fashioned cave homes in which to live. In northern China today, hundreds of thousands of people live in cave dwellings, comfortably cool in summer, snug and warm in winter.

Loess soil is fertile, easily worked even without a plow. But like all soil, loess needs moisture to produce crops, and rainfall in the valley is irregular. Sometimes it comes suddenly, in downpours, sometimes not at all when needed. Sometimes, reaching the floodplain swollen with water from melting mountain snows, the Yellow meets the first monsoon rains from the south and east. Devastating floods result. The Yellow River has aptly been named China's Sorrow.

Crumbling easily, loess soil easily erodes, to be picked up by the river. At the floodplain the Yellow River slows, dropping its silt, which settles to the bottom. Gradually the river bed rises and, finally, the Yellow shifts its course, making a new pathway to the sea. The Yellow River has changed its course more often than any other river in the world. Here in this great river valley, the Hsia Dynasty began under the Great Yu.

HSIA, SHANG, AND CHOU

Nothing is known directly about the Hsia Dynasty, ruled over for five hundred years by seventeen different kings. Archeologists have found no trace of it. What is known comes from the writings of ancient Chinese historians.

Yet most historians agree that the Hsia Dynasty, or something like it, must truly have existed. By 1500 B.C. for example, the Chinese had a well-developed written language. This is something which does not spring up overnight; written language evolves over centuries. Consequently, if a written Chinese language

Opposite: Ritual food vessel, made of bronze during the Shang Dynasty.

existed in 1500 B.C. it must have been developing for five hundred years or more. Some form of civilization must have existed in China long before 1500 B.C.

The Chinese developed not an alphabet, but a system of pictorial symbols called ideographs, each standing for an idea. The written language eventually came to contain about fifty thousand separate characters, written and read vertically rather than horizontally. Learning to write Chinese, then, required the memorization of many separate symbols, a long and arduous task. Still, this ideographic system would prove an important factor in unifying China. Northerners and southerners spoke entirely different dialects, making it impossible for them to converse. They could, however, easily communicate through common, standard, written symbols.

Hsia kings probably ruled over a group of city-states in what is now Shensi province, near the last great bend in the Yellow River. Most of the people probably lived in farming villages, growing millet as their main crop. Very likely they used bronze, a combination of tin and copper, to make tools and weapons. Historians draw this conclusion from the fact that by the next dynasty—the Shang—the art of working with bronze had reached a very high level.

No one knows how the Shang Dynasty began, although archeologists have found much evidence that it existed. They have dug up Shang figurines, vases, and other forms of pottery, as well as weapons and tools. The Shang probably changed their capital city from time to time, owing to war or to natural disasters such as floods. Diggings which began in 1929 near the modern Chinese city of Anyang uncovered what was probably the Shang capital city in about 1300 B.C. The city, laid out in squares, probably contained many government buildings, palaces, and temples. At the site near Anyang, archeologists found much evidence

of writing—on bronze, on bones, on pottery, and on jade and shells. It is possible that the people of the Shang Dynasty also wrote on wood, bamboo, and silk, although naturally no evidence of this survived. Shang soldiers used bronze weapons and rode into battle in chariots drawn by horses.

The Shang Dynasty ended around 1000 B.C. when a people known as Chou moved in from the west to conquer the people of the Yellow River valley. The Chou Dynasty would endure about eight hundred years.

Under the early Chou the land called China, although considerably larger than under the Shang, was nowhere near as extensive as it is today. The land extended from a little north of the Yellow River to portions along the Yangtze River to the south. It ran from mountains in the west to the sea. Later, the area was expanded north and west, but during the Chou period, not far south of the Yangtze.

By Chou times, certain Chinese ideas and ways of looking at the world had become established. Concepts concerning time, the family, and government were among these ideas, and they would persist throughout the history of traditional China.

IDEAS THAT SHAPED A PEOPLE

The Chinese do not seem to have troubled themselves with the questions of how or when time began. They were not concerned with how the universe got started, or when the earth was created. Of all the people historians have studied, the Chinese are the only people who have no story of creation. They possess no idea of a creator. To them, the universe and all within it simply existed, and always had; at some point heaven and earth separated, but it was of no particular importance when.

To the Chinese, natural time had no beginning and no end. It was circular. Days passed. Each point on earth met the sun each morning, and lost it as evening fell. The seasons came and went, year after year, without fail. All things on earth, man included, were part of nature, and man lived his life in harmony with nature, within the pulsating rhythm nature set. Man was part of nature, not above and apart from it.

According to the Chinese view, each individual received at birth both an animal and a spiritual soul. At death the animal soul remained with the corpse, gradually losing strength as the corpse decayed. The spiritual soul became a spirit. And spirits of ancestors could be of great assistance to members of the family still on earth. So could other spirits, such as those of rain and the soil, whose aid was essential to producing crops. Seeking help, and attempting to avoid disaster, Chinese families frequently made sacrifices of food and made requests to ancestors and to other spirits.

The Chinese family was more than simply mother, father, and children. It was an extended family, including grandparents and other close relatives on the father's side as well. The family also included members of the clan, made up of all blood relatives on the father's side. And families on earth were closely connected to the spiritual world through ancestors who had died and to the future through descendants as yet unborn. Those on earth owed their existence to their ancestors. They honored and respected them. And part of their obligation to their ancestors was to have children and maintain the family line. A man who did not was unfilial, lacking respect and reverence for ancestors and for parents.

Chinese society was a cluster of families and clans, and at the very top was the ruler, the head of all clans and families. In ancient times in China, the ruler was also the chief priest. He made sacrifices and requests to ancestors and heaven on behalf of all the people. He ruled with the Mandate of Heaven, the power

that Heaven, which meant nature, bestowed on him.

The Mandate of Heaven was granted to a ruler. If he did not rule justly and well, he ran the risk of losing Heaven's grace. The Mandate might be withdrawn, to be given to another. Probably the Mandate of Heaven idea dated from the period of the Chou, perhaps even from Shang times.

The Chinese ruler was not the descendant of a deity, but he ruled at the pleasure of the gods. The Mandate of Heaven concept became the Chinese way of explaining changes in dynasties —roughly speaking, ruling families. A ruler of any country must convince himself and his people that he is the lawful ruler. Otherwise, it becomes difficult for him to remain in power, for force alone will never long support a government. The Mandate of Heaven concept offered a lawful means of getting rid of a bad ruler and replacing him with a better one. Later, the concept came to include the idea that if a ruler did not rule wisely and well, the *people* had the Heaven-granted right to rebel against him. They would welcome a new ruler in his stead. If a rebellion was successful, the Mandate of Heaven idea explained why. If a rebellion did not succeed, the idea explained why it failed. "An unsuccessful rebel is a bandit, a successful one a king," ran a Chinese saying.

A PERIOD OF GREAT TURBULENCE

Although they claimed the Mandate of Heaven, Chou kings did not rule over a united China. In the beginning they divided the land up among friends, relatives, and nobles, assigning each an area called a state to govern. Lords who ruled the Chinese states were to be loyal to the Chou kings and pay them tribute, an annual tax. The Chou system of government is called feudalism. Under feudalism a central government, if one exists at all, is weak.

The Chou Dynasty gradually weakened as individual lords gained in strength. Then in 771 B.C., one powerful lord led an army against the Chou capital city, captured and destroyed it, and killed the Chou king. The remainder of the court fled for safety to the town of Loyang, in eastern China on the Yellow River. There the Chou remained, ruling over only a tiny patch of territory.

A long period of strife and turmoil followed, with troubles growing ever greater as the centuries passed. Each lord vied with others to expand his territory. Men won the right to rule a state through bribery, murder, and assassination. A ruler of one state might make a treaty of peace with the ruler of another and then, when it suited him, suddenly break the treaty. No one could be trusted. War, destruction, and uncertainty became the normal way of life.

AN AGE OF PHILOSOPHERS

This period of strife and turmoil caused much suffering among the Chinese people. It also produced philosophers who sought solutions to the problems of their times. Philosophers searched for principles to guide relationships between individuals, between individuals and nature, between individuals and groups, and between the people and their government. Some philosophers built on the past, while at the same time offering new ideas to guide ways of living. Others ignored the past, and simply developed new ideas to fit their time. So many philosophies appeared that the period became known as the age of the Hundred Schools. This simply meant that there were many different and competing sets of ideas offered on how to make the world a more orderly and peaceful place in which to live.

Kung Chiu was one philosopher among the many. Later he was called Kung Fu-tse, "the Master Philosopher Kung." Today he is known as Confucius.

Born in 551 B.C. in the state of Lu, located in the southwestern portion of what is now Shantung province, Confucius received a good education in ancient Chinese literature and ideas. His goal was to become the advisor of a ruler. Confucius wished to show a ruler how to govern well, how to establish peace and order in the midst of troubled times. "If some ruler would employ me," he said, "in a month I should have my system working. In three years everything would be running smoothly."

Confucius never realized his ambition. The king of Lu, it was said, was more interested in race horses and dancing girls than in listening to ideas about how to govern well. So Confucius left Lu to spend several years traveling from place to place in northern China. He taught and discussed ideas with whoever would gather round him. And he attracted many followers, rich and poor, young and old. But since Confucius never found a ruler who would listen to his ideas on how to govern, he died in 484 B.C. a disappointed man, in his own eyes a failure.

In his teaching, Confucius urged his pupils to look to the past for guidance. The past, he said, had been a time of order, peace, and tranquility. If such a period was to come once more, ancient wisdom must be taken as a guide.

Harmony lay at the heart of Confucius' thinking and teaching. Humans must live in harmony with both nature and each other, he said. How would harmony be achieved? According to Confucius, when everyone understood and accepted *li*, the idea of proper conduct and relationships among men.

One who understands li sees society as it is, composed of people with different abilities and status. There are superior people and inferior people. Some people are intelligent, others stupid. Some are wise, others simpleminded. Some are virtuous, others not. Some people are leaders, most are followers. Yet every person is capable of improvement, everyone can benefit from education.

Confucius believed that society was unequal. Every person had his proper place, according to his ability. Every person likewise had duties and responsibilities. If everyone accepted his place, his duties and responsibilities, he would understand li. Then there would be peace, order, and harmony in the world. If not, there would be suffering and chaos, which existed in Confucius' time.

Confucius stressed five relationships. One had to do with subjects and their ruler. All subjects were to respect and obey their ruler. In return, the ruler had to fulfill responsibilities, among which was to govern well, with justice, wisdom, and compassion. Later Confucian scholars stressed the idea that if a ruler did not govern well, the people had the right —even the duty—to rise against him and replace him with another.

In order to rule well, Confucius said, a ruler must achieve *jen*. This meant, among other things, love, kindness, charity, perfect virtue, compassion, and goodness. Only a ruler with jen, Confucius said, could set the proper tone for a country. "The people are the grass, the ruler like the wind; as the wind blows, so the grass bends."

Next to jen, *chih,* or wisdom, was the most important virtue. To achieve chih, one had to study the past and learn from ancient texts, and Confucius is said to have put together and edited several of these. Only by possessing wisdom could a person know which actions were right and proper. In addition, a person needed *yung,* the courage to make judgments and take right and proper action.

With respect to good government, according to Confucius, a good man ranked higher than laws in importance. Possessing jen, chih, and yung, a ruler could lead his people well. He need not force them to obey and be loyal to him, for the people would willingly and rightfully obey and respect a wise and virtuous ruler. "He who exercises government by means of his virtue may be compared to the north star, which keeps its place and all the stars turn around it," said Confucius.

"Do not do to others what you do not want others to do to you," Confucius said, speaking of proper relationships. And along with the relationship between ruler and those he ruled, Confucius stressed three relationships within the family—sons to fathers, wives to husbands, younger brothers to older ones. Fathers were superior. They were the rulers. They also possessed responsibility for caring for their wives and children. Women and children were inferior. Wives were to obey and respect husbands, and sons especially were to practice filial piety—they were to obey and respect parents, particularly the father. And younger sons were to defer to the wishes of older ones.

All females were considered inferior. As girls they were expected to help their mothers. When they reached the proper age, girls were to marry and go to live with their husband's family.

The fifth relationship of which Confucius spoke had to do with conduct between friends. Friendship, he said, should be based on love and mutual respect.

Confucius may have died a disappointed man, but no one had a greater influence than he on Chinese family life and society. Although Confucianism was really a code of ethics—a guide to conduct—it later became for all intents and purposes a religion. It formed a continuation of what has been called ancestor worship. Centuries after Confucius died, the whole system of education in China would be based on ideas he and his followers developed. Scholars educated in Confucian thought would be the officials who ran the government. They would be the most important and respected men in all of China.

IN LOVE WITH NATURE

Confucian scholars, it has been said, were in love with the past. Taoists, another group of philosophers and rivals of Confucians, were in love with nature.

Men should live in harmony with both nature and with other men, Confucians said. Said Taoists: men should concern themselves only with their relationships with nature. Society was man-made and evil. It offered nothing but suffering. Only by becoming one with nature could a person achieve happiness, said pessimistic and escapist Taoists.

Taoism began with Lao Tzu, who supposedly lived at the same time as Confucius. Historians disagree on whether there actually was a Lao Tzu. This may have been simply a name given to a group of men who developed Taoist ideas.

The basic ideas of Taoism are found in the *Tao Te Ching*—the Way and Its Power—reputedly written by Lao Tzu. Reading the *Tao Te Ching,* and meditating on it, one is directed to *Tao*—the Way, the Path, Nature. Each individual must seek Tao himself, away from other people, communicating alone with nature.

Taoists considered all things in nature related, man included. All were interdependent. There were no dividing points where one part of nature left off and another began. Wrote Chuang Tzu, a great Taoist scholar:

Long ago, Chuang Chou dreamed that he was a butterfly. He was elated as a butterfly—well pleased with himself, his aims satisfied. He knew nothing of Chou. But shortly he awoke and found himself to be Chou.

He did not know whether as Chou he dreamed he was a butterfly, or whether as a butterfly he dreamed he was Chou.

Emphasizing the unity of opposites, Taoists stressed the idea that if beauty was recognized, then ugliness must be present too. If there was goodness, there must also be evil. If respect was called for, then there was also disrespect. Accept life and human nature, said Taoists. Do not struggle. Think and reflect—but do not strain physically or mentally, for "He who stands on tiptoes does not stand on firm ground." Do not pursue knowledge, power, wealth, or a high place in society. All these are meaningless, unnatural, and harmful. Wealth breeds theft. Knowledge produces desires and therefore corruption. To create virtue simply means that there will be vice. Withdraw to nature and there seek Enlightenment, the Way. Wrote Lao Tzu:

To yield is to be preserved whole.
To bend is to become straight.
To be empty is to be full.
To be worn out is to be renewed.
To have little is to possess.
To have plenty is to be perplexed.

From the Taoist point of view, contrary to Confucian belief, government was as evil as any other part of society. The ideal ruler to Taoists was not one who possessed jen, acting wisely and justly. He was one who would accomplish everything by doing nothing. "The one who knows does not speak, and the one who speaks does not know," wrote Lao Tzu.

Taoism was a purely individualistic philosophy. Each person could derive his own meaning from the words in *Tao Te Ching*. And each time he read it, he could well discover a new meaning in the words. Each person discovered his own individual Way.

Confucianism and Taoism flourished side by

side in China. Confucianism served as a guide to learning, family relationships, and government. Taoism remained a philosophy for individuals. A person could be both Confucian and Taoist at one and the same time. It was later said that a person was a Confucian while he held a government office, a Taoist when he left it. Taoism and Confucianism could appeal to two sides of the same individual.

Chinese literature is full of stories illustrating Confucianist and Taoist points of view. One, for example, is "The Sparrow and the Phoenix." Another is "Horses' Hoofs." It is not difficult to determine which story reflects which philosophy.

One time a small, ugly sparrow laid three eggs in her nest on the ground. While she was away from the nest for just a minute, a field mouse came by and stole two of the eggs.

When the sparrow returned she was heartbroken. She flew off to make a charge against the field mouse before the Queen of the Birds, the phoenix, who should have been as wise as she was powerful.

Now, the proud phoenix didn't want to waste time over a plain sparrow, so she said crossly, "Can't you see I am busy? Further-

Gold phoenix made during the T'ang period.

more, it is up to parents to look out for their own children. If a field mouse robbed your nest it must have been because you were careless."

"As Queen of the Birds, how can you turn me away? Nothing happening to your tiniest subject should be unimportant to you. However, if you do not consider my problem worthy of your attention, be prepared in case something should happen to you."

The phoenix let the sparrow scold on and on. Finally the poor sparrow saw that she was wasting her breath. She flew home. She took a sharp twig and made it into a spear. Then she lighted on a tree above her nest and waited for the greedy field mouse.

When he came for the last egg, the sparrow was very angry. She flew down and jabbed his eye with her sharp spear. The pain was so terrible that the field mouse whipped around and around blindly, squeaking loudly. In his pain he darted into the nostril of a lion lying asleep by the shore. Startled from his nap, the lion jumped into the water, thinking that a giant bee had flown into his nose.

Underwater was a dragon. To avoid being eaten by the lion, the dragon jumped completely out of the water and by accident brushed against the nest of the phoenix herself, and tipped over her precious egg.

Now the phoenix was angry beyond reason. She confronted the dragon and scolded, "Dragon, you live in water while I live on land. Now you jump out of the water and break the only egg I have laid this year! What is your excuse?"

"Phoenix, I am so sorry to have broken your only egg. A lion dove into the water and frightened me so that I jumped out and accidentally knocked over your nest. Go blame the lion."

When the phoenix went to scream at the lion, he replied, "Phoenix, you must not blame me. I was minding my own business, sleeping by the seashore, when a field mouse ran into my nose and frightened me. I dove into the water because I thought he was a giant bee. Go yell at the field mouse."

When the phoenix confronted the field mouse, he answered, "Please don't blame me. I was going by the sparrow's nest when she flew down like a mad bird and jabbed me in the eye with a spear. My eye was smarting with pain. By mistake I darted blindly into the lion's nostril. It is the sparrow's fault. Go speak to her."

"Yes, Queen of the Birds," said the sparrow. "I am directly responsible for your loss. However, didn't you tell me that parents are responsible for their own, and that if anything happened to the eggs it was most likely because the mother was careless? You did not comfort me when my two eggs were broken, so how can you expect my sympathy for your one broken egg? Do leave me alone."

At this the phoenix was most sad. She could do nothing else but fly away and weep.

HORSES' HOOFS

Horses have hoofs to carry them over frost and snow, and hair to protect them from wind and cold. They eat grass and drink water, and fling up their tails and gallop. Such is the real nature of horses. Ceremonial halls and big dwellings are of no use to them.

One day Polo, a famous horse trainer, appeared, saying, "I am good at managing horses." So he burned their hair and clipped them, and pared their hoofs and branded them. He put halters around their necks and shackles around their legs and numbered

Horse and groom from the T'ang Dynasty.

them according to their stables. The result was that two or three in every ten died. Then he kept them hungry and thirsty, trotting them and galloping them, and taught them to run in formations, with the misery of the tasselled bridle in front and the fear of the knotted whip behind, until more than half of them died.

The potter says, "I am good at managing clay. If I want it round, I use compasses; if rectangular, a square." The carpenter says, "I am good at managing wood. If I want it curved, I use an arc; if straight, a line." But on what grounds can we think that the nature of clay and wood desires this application of compasses and square, and arc and line? Nevertheless, every age praises Polo for his skill in training horses, and potters and carpenters for their skill with clay and wood. Those who manage the affairs of the empire make the same mistake.

. . . Horses live on dry land, eat grass, and drink water. When pleased, they rub their necks together. When angry, they turn round and kick up their heels at each other.

Thus far only do their natural instincts carry them. But bridled and bitted, with a moon-shaped metal plate on their foreheads, they learn to cast vicious looks, to turn their heads to bite, to nudge at the yoke, to cheat the bit out of their mouths or steal the bridle off their heads. Thus their minds and gestures become like those of thieves. This is the fault of Polo.

In older days, the people did nothing in particular at their homes and went nowhere in particular in their walks. Having food, they rejoiced; tapping their bellies, they wandered about. Thus far the natural capacities of the people carried them. The Wisemen came then to make them bow and bend with ceremonies and music, in order to regulate their relationships. They dangled charity and duty before them, in order to keep their minds in submission. Then the people began to labor and develop a taste for knowledge, and to struggle with one another in their desire for gain, to which there is no end. This is the error of the Wisemen.

A CIVILIZATION FLOWERS

The long period of war and destruction in China came to an end early in the third century B.C. The century before, rulers of the intensely warlike state of Ch'in had sent their armies eastward to conquer neighboring kingdoms. By 221 B.C., the Ch'in had subdued all of China north of the Yangtze River. The Ch'in king became Shih Huang Ti —the First Emperor. Under him the land ceased to be one of several small kingdoms. It became an empire, called China after the Ch'in.

Giving China its name, Shih Huang Ti also gave China its first central government. He abolished all laws of the separate kingdoms, replacing them with laws that applied to all Chinese. He divided the land into districts, each ruled by a military governor who reported directly to the emperor.

Determined to prevent rebellion, Shih Huang Ti moved 120,000 noble families from many parts of China west to Shensi, the original Ch'in area. There he could keep an eye on them.

Shih Huang Ti had roads built outward from his capital city, Ch'ang-an, so that, if necessary, his armies could move quickly in every direction. He also had numerous canals dug to connect rivers. To protect China from barbarian tribes in the north, Shih Huang Ti ordered that the Great Wall be constructed along China's northern boundary. Over the years several short stretches of wall had been built; now they were connected to form a barrier continuous for fourteen hundred miles. Tens of thousands of men were forced to labor on this stupendous project, erecting a wall fourteen feet high and forty feet thick. It was said that a million died, that each stone in the Great Wall cost a human life.

Further to unify China, Shih Huang Ti insisted that the written characters of the Chinese language be made standard throughout the land. There might be several ways of speaking Chinese, several dialects. There would, however, be only one way to write it.

Few of Shih Huang Ti's changes were made without opposition. He burned books, and for this scholars hated him. Peasants hated him for the heavy taxes they had to pay, for army service they had to give, and for the labor they were forced to perform on canals and roads. Members of noble families hated him because he had destroyed their kingdoms and their power. Shih Huang Ti died in 210 B.C. His son ruled for only a few years. Then a rebellion, led by a peasant who became the founder of the Han Dynasty, destroyed the Ch'in Dynasty.

The changes Shih Huang Ti had made,

Opposite: Wooden figure of a Buddhist saint, carved during the Yüan period.

though, were not undone. The next dynasty, the Han, built on them, made further changes, and Chinese civilization flowered.

MEN OF HAN

Beginning in 206 B.C., the Han Dynasty marked a great period in Chinese history, especially during the fifty-three-year reign of Han Wu Ti, who became emperor in 140 B.C. Wrote the historian Ssu-ma Ch'ien about Han Wu Ti and the Han:

By the time the present emperor had been on the throne a few years, a period of over seventy years had passed since the foundation of the Han Dynasty. During that time the country had met with no major disturbances. Except in times of flood or drought, every person was well supplied. Every family had enough to get along on. The granaries in the city and the countryside were full. The government treasuries were running over with wealth. In the central granary of the government new grain was heaped on top of the old until the building was full. The grain overflowed and piled up outside.

The Han Dynasty witnessed great advances in learning and in education. Books long hidden from the book burners of the Ch'in Dynasty were brought out, copied, and assembled into libraries. The sayings of Confucius, and scholars' writings about them and other Confucian ideas, became the basis for education in China. One Confucian school began in 84 B.C. with fifty students. By the end of the Han period, in A.D. 220, the school enrolled thirty thousand students. Historians such as Ssu-ma Ch'ien used the Confucian classics and other ancient writings to construct histories of past dynasties. They drew on their own ob-

servations and documents to write histories of Han times. Besides histories, a great deal of poetry and other literature was produced.

In about A.D. 100 the Chinese invented papermaking. They developed water clocks that kept accurate time. Following careful observations of the stars and planets, they reckoned the length of a year at 365.25 days. They worked out a calendar that long remained official. Mathematicians used the place value system. Although they did not use the zero, they left an empty space for it in their calculations. The arts of making porcelain—glazed pottery—and weaving silk and working with jade reached new heights. All this occurred during the four hundred years of the Han.

The Emperor Han Wu Ti extended the Chinese borders. More land was taken in southern China and western boundaries were pushed into Tibet and Central Asia. Parts of Korea and what is now Vietnam came under Chinese control. The Han did not rule such areas as Korea and Vietnam directly. So long as the rulers of those areas paid tribute to the emperor, and did not try to rebel against the Chinese, they were allowed to conduct their own affairs.

General peace and unity marked many of the years of the Han Dynasty. The period was also important as a time during which the Chinese began to think of themselves as a people separate from all others, well advanced in learning and in civilization, a special group. They were proud men of Han, the people of the Middle Kingdom, occupying the center of the world. They were self-sufficient, having no need of products or ideas from anywhere else on earth. Chinese under the Han became a strong and confident people. There would be other times when China was disunited, but, after the Han, its culture would persist regardless of who ruled the land. There would now and then be foreign influences on China, but these would be changed and made Chinese. In that sense, China was like a vast sea that salted all the rivers flowing into it.

Confucian scholars in China did much to further this feeling of confidence, unity, and exclusiveness. It was they who shared a common written language, standardized under the Ch'in Dynasty. It was they who kept alive ancient literature and learning and built on it. And, under the Han, it was Confucian scholars who ran the government.

END OF THE HAN

All dynasties come to an end. The Han was no exception. During the second century A.D. there were years of drought, famine, and flood, and epidemics of disease. Suffering, hardship, and disorder increased. There were conflicts within the government, and the Han no longer were able to control the country. To many people, all these were signs that the dynasty would soon fall, that the Mandate of Heaven would be withdrawn. The year 184, people said, would be the year in which a new dynasty would sweep away the Han.

In central China, where epidemics had been especially bad, there arose a man who insisted that he could save the people. He was Chang Chueh, a Taoist magician who preached the Way of the Great Peace. He claimed that by pronouncing magic words over pure water, he could change the liquid into a medicine that would cure disease. Chang Chueh also assured all who followed him that they could never be killed by arrow, lance, or sword.

Thousands of peasants flocked to Chang Chueh as their savior. He organized them into the Yellow Turbans, the name taken from the yellow kerchiefs they wore around their heads in battle. The fighting was to begin on April 14, 184, when Chang Chueh planned to lead his people in a great rebellion. The plot was discovered. Chang Chueh escaped, though, and began to organize rebellion once again.

This time the government, acting with great force, killed more than 500,000 Yellow Turbans.

Crushing the Yellow Turban rebellion did not save the Han Dynasty, however. After further rebellions the dynasty finally ended in the year 220.

China now broke into small, warring kingdoms once again. There were invasions from the north. The fall of the Han signalled the beginning of a period of nearly four hundred years during which there would be little save turmoil, strife, and uncertainty in China.

FLOCKING TO RELIGIONS

At an earlier time, during a long period of chaos and conflict, great philosophies had developed. Now, during a similar period, two great religions flourished in China. One was Taoism, the other Buddhism.

As a popular religion, Taoism rested on ideas developed by men who followed Lao Tzu. But the religion was also well mixed with magic and with alchemy. Alchemists believed they could find a drug or a mixture that would make a person live forever, or at the very least, a mixture that could be used to change ordinary metal into gold. From alchemy, eventually, the science of chemistry developed. Common people who adopted Taoism added certain practices to that philosophy. They worshipped spirits and believed in ghosts and magic charms. They confessed sins, recited Taoist sayings, and took part in nature ceremonies.

Working with alchemy, Taoist priests were led to discover herbs and minerals that actually did help cure disease. They also discovered the magnetic compass and gunpowder. But Confucian scholars looked down on popular Taoism. They considered the religion merely a big bundle of superstitious nonsense, pooh-poohing alchemy and magic. Some historians have suggested that this may be one reason why respect for science and technology never took hold among the traditional Chinese.

During the time of warring kingdoms, Confucian scholars lost much of their power and importance. Later they became powerful once again, controlling the government and the system of education. From the Confucian point of view, the true scholar concerned himself with books, learning, literature, and history. Science and technology could well be left to magicians and tricksters, which is what Confucians considered Taoists to be.

Certainly the Taoists did not utilize the full potential of their inventions. Compasses were used to find proper spots for graves. Gunpowder was used to make firecrackers to scare away evil spirits, later to enliven festivals and celebrations.

Buddhism, which found its way to China from India in the first century A.D., during the Han Dynasty, became a great rival of Taoism among the people. Eventually, Buddhism was an immensely popular religion. In north China, by A.D. 400, possibly nine out of ten families were Buddhist. One hundred years later, it was said, all Chinese were Buddhist.

Founded by Prince Gautama Siddhartha, who was born in 573 B.C., original Buddhism was a pessimistic religion. It viewed life as a time of suffering and sorrow, of poverty, misery, famine, pestilence, and death. Human desire, Gautama said, brought on such suffering. If a person was to escape misery, he must overcome desire, purge himself of it and become indifferent to the world. He could accomplish this only through rigid mental and physical discipline and meditation. Eventually a person could achieve *nirvana*. He would know peace, freedom from desire, and an end to suffering. Nirvana was not heaven, but a state of mind. Attaining it, a person found Enlightenment.

Buddhism rested on the idea of reincarnation—that all creatures, humans and others, upon death were reborn in another form, again and again. The form of reincarnation each time depended on the amount of merit a creature had accumulated in his previous existence. Between rebirths there was a resting time. This was a sort of holiday for those creatures who had done well in the previous existence, a hell for those who had done badly. Reaping little or no merit condemned a person to rebirth as a lower animal than he had been. Having accumulated great merit, a creature might be reborn as one of the highest animals, a human. The Buddhist goal, however, was not simply to acquire merit. The objective was to end reincarnation—which, whether a person was born or reborn human or not, simply meant endless suffering. When a person achieved nirvana he ended this cycle; there was no more rebirth, no more suffering of any kind.

Pessimistic about life, Buddhism nonetheless was based on love and respect for all living creatures. A person "must cultivate a heart of love that knows no anger, that knows no ill will," said Prince Gautama. A person must be charitable, helpful, and generous, most of all avoiding hatred. "Hatred does not cease by hatred at any time," Gautama said. "Hatred ceases by love." Further, Buddhists did not recognize man as a creature apart from nature. He was very much in nature, but only a small part of a larger, awe-inspiring whole.

The Chinese changed Buddhism from a religion of endlessly recited prayers and strict discipline to one more of simple faith and love. Nirvana became heaven. Sects like the Pure Land, which emphasized pageantry and faith, flourished among the Chinese. The Chinese version of Buddhism became immensely popular during the period of constant civil war. In times of turmoil and confusion, people customarily flock to a faith that offers hope, comfort, and a promise of eventual rest.

No other foreign influence had as much

effect on China as Buddhism. The Chinese language gained new words. New forms of literature appeared. Buddhist chants enriched Chinese music. While Confucianism centered an ordinary citizen's attention on the family, Buddhism tended to broaden this point of view. It upheld the ideas of aid and charity and love for all people. Buddhism influenced Taoism, infusing it with the idea of reincarnation. Taoists also adopted the Buddhist belief that there were thirty-three heavens and eighteen hells.

Buddhists were responsible for the invention of printing with wood blocks in China. This probably occurred in the 800s, long before the idea of printing was born anywhere else in the world.

For a time Buddhism was the most popular religion in China. This did not mean, however, that every Chinese Buddhist was only that and nothing more. For many Chinese, ideas from several religions and philosophies could blend together. A man could be a Confucianist in public, a Taoist in private, and still look favorably on some Buddhist concepts.

In 590, with the beginning of the Sui Dynasty, the long period of division in China came to a close. Under the Sui, invaders were driven from the land and fortifications on the northern border were strengthened. New canals and roads were constructed. Like the Ch'in before it, the Sui Dynasty united China and gave it a central government. Also like the Ch'in, the Sui did not last long. Yang Ti, the second Sui emperor, destroyed his father's work. He was extravagant, fighting unnecessary and costly wars in Korea. Yang Ti ruled the people harshly, and the Sui Dynasty soon fell, in 618. But like the Ch'in, which had prepared the path for the Han, the Sui prepared the way for the T'ang. This dynasty would last three hundred years.

Under the T'ang, Confucian scholars regained their influence in government. Under the Sung Dynasty, which followed the T'ang, scholars strengthened their power, retaining it down to modern times. The Confucian way of thinking was the traditional Chinese way of thinking. Scholar-officials set the tone for the entire country. They composed the bureaucracy, the vast corps of government officials. Their tasks were to administer the tax, educational, and judicial systems, see after the building and maintenance of canals and roads, and develop and administrate government policy.

The Chinese symbol of heaven, made of jade during the Chou Dynasty.

SCHOLAR-OFFICIALS

Fan Chin was a poor man, but he wanted desperately to be something better. He wished to pass the emperor's examinations and become a scholar-literatus, an official. He tried the first time, and failed, when he was twenty. He tried the twentieth time, and passed, when he was fifty-four. Much of the time his father-in-law, a butcher, had supported him, though looking down on Fan Chin as a lazy, good-for-nothing fellow.

When news arrived that he had passed, Fan Chin fainted. Revived, he let out a loud laugh, clapped his hands, and shouted, "Aha! I've passed! I've passed!" Then he ran wildly out of the house and fell into a muddy pond.

Fan Chin's life now changed. "He may be my son-in-law," said Butcher Hu, "but he's an official now—one of the stars of heaven." The neighbors all paid him honor. Chang Chin-chai, a rich landlord in the town, came to call on Fan Chin. He awarded Fan Chin fifty pieces of silver to show his deep respect and offered him a fine new house by the town's east gate, with three courtyards with three rooms in each.

Other people presented Fan Chin with land. He had servants now. He had money and rice. His wife could dress in fine clothes. Fan Chin had leaped from the lower class into the very highest class of men in China. He had brought honor to himself, his family, and his village.

This story, from the novel *The Scholars* by Wu Ching-tzu, written in the eighteenth century, poked gentle fun at the examination system and scholar-officials, also known as scholar-literati. Humor aside, though, scholar-officials were the rulers of traditional China. And, theoretically at least, anyone, be he rich or poor, could become a scholar-literatus by passing the examinations.

THEORY VS. PRACTICE

Of course, practice did not always square with theory. Few peasant boys from poor families ever reached the upper class along the examination route. Schooling cost money, and few peasant families could afford it. Wealthy landowners as well as merchants in some cases bought passing marks for their sons through bribery and influence. Some officials themselves were exceedingly corrupt. Probably a number were shallow, narrow-minded individuals—education does not broaden everyone. Undoubtedly some were poor administrators, hanging onto their positions only through bribery and influence. Competition to pass examinations was in-

Opposite: Self-portrait of Shen-Chou, an artist and scholar of the Ming Dynasty.

tense, a whole life style hanging in the balance. Aside from government employment, traditional China offered few avenues to success. China was far from an open society in which existed numerous paths to prominence and security. It would seem natural therefore that some applicants, at least, would resort to almost any means to achieve their goal. Once in government office, retaining a post and winning promotion depended much on the favor of one's superior. Consequently, that underlings should bestow gifts on superiors at every opportunity is not surprising.

Landscape with waterfall, a hanging scroll painted by Wên Chêng-ming in the sixteenth century.

Passing gifts to government officials probably reflected in part the Chinese pattern of mutual dependence. Members of the family, inferior and superior, depended on each other. So did subordinates and superiors in government. Yet gift-giving and palm-crossing, which greased the give-and-take of government, business, and other relationships, were seldom conducted in secret, under the table. It was an accepted fact of life that public office carried with it certain rewards as well as powers, and that one should help his friends and relatives and expect favors in return. And since government policy affected most groups, it paid a person to learn to work with officials with the least possible amount of friction. No government has ever been entirely free of favor and special treatment, regardless of the fact that according to the values of certain cultures such activity spells corruption. The Chinese, perhaps, simply adopted a lenient and workable attitude toward human nature; at least that probably was the traditional Chinese point of view.

THE MAKING OF A SCHOLAR

On the whole, the unique Chinese system of selecting bureaucrats on the basis of examination and Confucian philosophy worked well. If nothing else, the fact that it endured for centuries indicates that. An education consisting mainly of the study and memorization of Confucian classics had little direct bearing on bureaucratic duties. But such schooling was supposed to educate a man, instill in him proper attitudes, and impart to him a certain degree of wisdom. Su Tung-po, who lived at about the midpoint of the Sung Dynasty, in the eleventh century, exemplified what a scholar-literatus was supposed to be.

Far up the Yangtze River, in western China, at the foot of high Omei Mountain, the Min

River joins the larger stream. A short distance upstream on the Min lies the town of Meishan. Here, on a December day in 1036, Su Tung-po was born, the elder son of a family that, though not rich, was fairly well off. The Su family owned land and a fine house, and it employed two servants. Later, another son, Tse-yu, was born. Along with a grandfather, the Su family now contained five members.

When he was six, Su Tung-po entered elementary school. There he mastered the difficult art and skill of writing and reading the Chinese language. A Taoist priest kept the school Su attended, which held more than a hundred pupils. Su Tung-po's family was Buddhist.

At age eleven Su entered the secondary school, beginning now to prepare for the official district examinations. Success there would lead to examinations given every three years in the emperor's palace in the capital city of Kaifeng. Su Tung-po studied ancient Confucian writings as well as histories, poetry, and other literature. Students in those schools did not simply read and then write about or discuss what they had read. They had to memorize large sections of books and be able to recite them word for word. This meant many long hours of hard and tedious work. But Su Tung-po's ambition was to pass the examinations and become a scholar-literatus, a member of the highest and most respected and influential class in all of China.

EXAMINATION TIME

His studies completed at age eighteen, Su Tung-po considered himself prepared. First of all, however, his parents found him a wife, fifteen-year-old Wang Fu, who lived with her parents in Chingshen, a town about fifteen miles away. Following Chinese custom, Su Tung-Po and Wang Fu did not meet until the wedding ceremony, but afterward they fell in love and the marriage was a good one.

Having passed district examinations, soon after his marriage Su Tung-po set out for the capital with his younger brother Tse-yu and their father, arriving there in May 1056. Until fall, when the preliminary examinations were given, they resided in a Buddhist temple. In the autumn, among the forty-five candidates from Meishan, thirteen passed, the Su brothers among them. These thirteen would remain in Kaifeng until the following spring, when they would take the final examinations.

For Su Tung-po and the others, long years of study and memory work had pointed to this one great day. If they failed, they could take the examinations over, trying as often as they wished. But until they passed the examinations, their lives would have little meaning. Even if they passed, they might have to wait for some time for an appointment to a government job, and if they did not get one, they could only be teachers, and poorly paid. Consequently, passing the examinations, then getting a government position, were tremendously important.

On examination day the Su brothers arose before daylight so as to be at the palace by dawn, taking cold meals with them, for they could not leave until the examinations were completed. During the entire time they would be locked in separate cubicles and closely guarded, to eliminate opportunity for cheating. Once finished, their papers would be copied by clerks, then coded with a number. The elder scholars who read and marked the papers would not know who had written them, minimizing the chance of favoritism.

The two brothers first had to respond to questions on history and on principles of good government. Then they had an examination on the writings and wisdom of Confucius. Next they were examined on poetry. Finally, they had to write an essay on government.

Su Tung-po did something a candidate seldom did, and he got away with it. He invented a story as part of his essay on government.

In the time of the Emperor Yao, he wrote, a man was about to be condemned to death. "Three times the minister of justice said, 'Let him be killed!'" Su Tung-po wrote, "and three times Emperor Yao said, 'Let him be pardoned!'"

Scholars who read the examination papers had never heard of that story. But none of them cared to admit it, for they were supposed to know everything. So no one questioned it then, but some time later curiosity got the better of one old scholar. He said to Su Tung-po:

"By the way, where does that story occur about Emperor Yao and the minister of justice? I can't quite recall where I read it."

"I invented it," Su replied.

"You did!" exclaimed the scholar.

"Well, that was what the wise emperor would have done, wasn't it?" asked Su. The young scholar was a Confucian from start to finish.

Su Tung-po had an excellent imagination, and he became a famous poet. But this incident revealed one thing about him. He found it impossible to work entirely within the system.

On April 18, 1057, both Su brothers passed the examination, two among 388 successful candidates. Six days later, they were declared scholar-literati, among the most honored group in China.

THE FIRST APPOINTMENT

Su Tung-po received a government appointment as an assistant magistrate, a person who was both an administrator and a judge. So did his brother. Su Tung-po won assignment to the town of Fengshiang, along the Wei River in western China. There his main duty was to travel throughout a certain area settling disputes between persons which could not be settled by local village or town elders. After three years in the west, Su was brought back to Kaifeng and given a job in the emperor's library.

The next year Su Tung-po's wife died, followed in death in 1066 by his father. The Su brothers now left their posts to take the bodies of father and wife a thousand miles back home for burial. There they remained for twenty-seven months, according to Confucian custom.

After the mourning period, Su Tung-po returned to the capital. There he soon found himself in trouble.

IN AND OUT OF TROUBLE

Controversy arose among the scholar-official advisors to the emperor over new tax and peasant loan procedures proposed by the premier, or chief official, Wang An-shih. Wang An-shih proposed that peasants be allowed to borrow money from the government when they needed it to buy seeds in the spring or food to last until harvest. They could thus avoid going to moneylenders to borrow at high interest rates. Further, he wished to tax people according to their ability to pay, not at a flat rate applied equally to all. Finally, Wang An-shih proposed that peasants be allowed to pay taxes in money instead of rice if they wished.

Scholar-literati calling themselves innovators lined up behind Wang An-shih. Those who wished no change at all called themselves conservatives. The censors, men whose job was to monitor the performance of bureaucrats and who could freely criticize government actions, supported the conservative side before the emperor.

As a librarian, Su Tung-po had no need to inject himself into the quarrel. He did so anyway, adopting the conservative line and writing several letters to the emperor criticizing

Wang An-shih's proposals. The censors' criticism did not please Wang An-shih, the "Bull-Headed Premier," and neither did Su Tung-po's. The innovators won the argument, changes were made, and Wang An-shih enjoyed revenge. He arranged for Su Tung-po to be removed from his library job and sent south as an assistant magistrate to the city of Hang-chow. Later he was sent to Suchow.

At Suchow Su Tung-po made his name as an efficient administrator during a Yellow River flood which threatened to crumble the city's wall, the only protection against disaster. As well-to-do families prepared to flee Suchow, Su Tung-po turned them back, urging on them the wisdom that their departure would only create panic in the city. Then, using thousands of laborers and working day and night himself, Su Tung-po managed to save the wall and have it built higher. After threatening Suchow for forty-five days, the Yellow River went down. The emperor himself congratulated Su Tung-po for his work and granted him money to build a permanent dam against the Yellow along the southeastern part of the city.

Thanks to his ability to govern and his poetry, Su Tung-po was now known as the first scholar of the land, called "Master" by scholar-literati throughout China. Even so, he was not to avoid trouble.

Wang An-shih was no longer part of the government, but many of the innovators still were in office and they liked Su Tung-po no more than ever. He had as little use for them. Su believed that as a government official he served the emperor and the people first, himself second. He did not think all officials felt that way. Some, he concluded, were mainly interested in playing politics, interested first of all in keeping their jobs, only secondarily in performing their tasks well. And Su Tung-po let his dislike of some officials show in certain poems he wrote. He compared some of them to croaking frogs, others to chirping locusts, and still others to owls and chickens. He even referred to certain ones as monkeys. Su

Tung-po was not a man to let matters ride and bide his time.

The men Su Tung-po ridiculed finally struck back, having him arrested for criticizing the government and insulting the emperor. After a trial, Su Tung-po was found guilty. The emperor, however, refused to punish him severely. He was sentenced to live near Hang-chow, on the Yangtze, forbidden to move from there without the emperor's permission. Wrote Su:

In all my life, writing has brought me into trouble. From now on the lesser my fame, the better it is for me.

Su Tung-po's fame did not diminish, however, nor did his writing cease. He remained first scholar of the land. But for several years he lived as a farmer and enjoyed the rural life, continuing to write poetry and studying Buddhism and Taoism. Content to live out his life as a farmer, Su expressed himself in this way:

Last year I cleared the rubble on the Eastern Slope,
And planted myself mulberries a hundred yards long.
This year I cut the hay to thatch the Snow Hall.
Exposed to the sun and wind, my face becomes well tanned.

THE FINAL YEARS

Twenty years after the conservative-innovator controversy over government policy, a new emperor came to the throne. Abolishing changes the innovators had made, he brought the conservatives back into power, at the same time recalling Su Tung-po to the capital. Su returned, reluctantly, voicing his thoughts in a poem, speaking somewhat like a Taoist:

Let me go home—
But where is my home? . . .
Human affairs shift and change like a
  shuttle.
Let me take time to gaze
At the clear ripples on the Lo stream in the
  autumn wind.
To kind remembrance of me,
Spare the gentle twigs of Snow Hall's
  willow.
And I pray my friends across the river
To come at times and sun my fishing rain-
  coat.

During the next several years Su Tung-po held numerous government posts and at one time served as secretary to the emperor, at another as teacher of the royal family. But Su did not care for palace life. He did not like court politics, preferring the life of an official in the provinces. Finally appointed a provincial governor of Hangchow, he got his wish.

As governor, Su improved Hangchow's water supply. He had a hospital built. He did much to make the city beautiful, enhancing it with lakes and gardens. During floods of the Yangtze, he put in many long hours caring for the people. And during those times of flood, he severely criticized officials in the capital for not giving him the aid he asked for and for not taking other steps he recommended. Su Tung-po's sharp and impatient letters annoyed the officials, and since Su wrote letters to the emperor too, the officials had to explain themselves to him. This annoyed them even more.

The fact that Su Tung-po had served well as governor did not help him when the government changed once again, when the emperor decided to bring the innovators back. The conservatives now were out and all conservatives, including Su Tung-po's brother, Tse-yu, lost their jobs and were given lesser ones. Su

Tung-po was made a magistrate far in the south of China, in Canton.

Here Su had little to do officially. So he continued to write and study Taoism, at the same time enjoying life in the pleasant climate of South China. In the innovators' eyes, Su was too well off, and he was finally ordered to the island of Hainan, off the coast of China. Here the climate was damp, foggy in winter, and very humid in summer. Still, Su, now sixty years old, had not lost his perspective or his sense of humor. He wrote to a friend:

I have been in this place over half a year and can somehow get along. I need not go into the details. Think of me as a [Buddhist] monk who has been driven out of the Ling-ying Temple and is now living in a small cottage, eating simple peasant meals! I can live my life this way to the end of my days. As to malaria and other diseases, are there not diseases in the north? One can die of all kinds of diseases and not of malaria only. It is true, there are no doctors around this place, but think how many people are killed annually by doctors at the capital! I know you will laugh when you read this, and cease to worry about me. When friends ask about me, just tell them what I have said.

Once again the death of an emperor changed Su Tung-po's life, and in 1100 the new emperor called him back to China. But he now had only a short time to live. Ill with malaria, Su Tung-po died in July 1101.

As a scholar-official, Su Tung-po had led an up-and-down life. He had served well in every post he held. But he never mastered the art of politics, unable to still his pen, unable to remain quiet and wait. He was inclined to be outspoken, and impatient with what struck him as stupidity, regardless of whether it was a conservative or an innovator who displayed it.

Yet, as far as he himself was concerned, Su Tung-po had lived a full life. He had written much fine poetry, and many works on Confucianism, Taoism, and Buddhism. He had, to the best of his ability, remained true to the Confucian principles he had mastered through long hours of study as a youth. Said Lin Yutang, who nearly one thousand years later wrote the story of Su Tung-po's life, *The Gay Genius*: "Su Tung-po died and his name is only a memory, but he has left behind for all of us the joys of his spirit and the pleasures of his mind, and these are imperishable."

A FLOWERING

The Sung Dynasty, which began in 960 and lasted about three hundred years, marked a high point in traditional Chinese culture. The Sung Dynasty was known especially for painters of insects, birds and fish, flowers and bamboos, cottages and palaces, and figures of men. Sung landscapes in particular were magnificent. Influenced by Buddhism and Taoism, Chinese art of the time has been called a "cosmic inspiration; a feeling of closeness between the human spirit and the energies of the elements—the winds, the mists, the soaring peaks, the plunging torrents." Philosopher Shao Yung, who lived during the Sung, is said to have remarked: "I am happy because I am human, and not an animal; a male, and not a female; a Chinese, and not a barbarian; and because I live in Loyang, the most wonderful city in all the world."

Li Ch'ing-chao, who lived between 1081 and 1140, proved to be the foremost literary woman in Chinese history. Daughter of a life-long friend of Su Tung-po, Li Ch'ing-chao contributed a great deal of poetry to Chinese literature. In her "To the Tune of 'A Sprig of Plum Blossom'" she lamented the death of her husband:

The fragrance of the pink lotos falls, the jade
  mat hints of autumn.
Softly I unfasten my silk cloak
And enter the boat alone.
Who is sending a letter from among the
  clouds?
When the swan message returns, the balcony
  is flooded with moonlight.
The blossoms drift on, the water flows.
There is the same yearning of the heart,
But it abides in two places.
There is no way to drive away this yearning.
Driven from the eyebrows [knit together in
  sorrow],
It enters the heart.

Chinese drama had bare beginnings during the Han Dynasty; it did not fully develop until the Yüan Dynasty which, beginning in 1260, followed the Sung. Typically all players were male. Their costumes were elaborate and costly. Actors were made up and costumed to symbolize the characters they portrayed. A general, for example, wore a headdress of long, sweeping pheasant feathers. A young scholar always carried a fan. Action took place on a stage bare of scenery, props, and curtain; actors had to create all the illusion of the play themselves. Ordinarily the script was in verse and much of it was sung, the voices accompanied by musical instruments. Many of the plays were based on historical incidents or stories, frequently dating from Han times or earlier.

CUSTOMS AND TRADITIONS

Scholar-literati were the poets, the philosophers, the playwrights. As the upper class, they ruled traditional China. The peasantry, making up 85 to 90 percent of the population, supported China. The peasantry was China and the Chinese peasant, like natural time, went on forever. He tilled the soil, producing the country's wheat, rice, and millet. When the government ordered it, he labored to build roads, bridges, and palaces for emperors. In wartime he was the soldier in the emperor's army. Year in, year out, he paid taxes to support the bureaucracy and the government. There were always many more of his kind than any other group in China, and some of those who did not work with their hands tended to look down on him.

To the Chinese peasant, land and family, intertwined, were the most important things in life. Land did not belong to the individual. It belonged to the family, to all generations. It belonged to the living, to ancestors, and to those yet unborn. A broken family was one whose land was gone, a family that had lost a vital link connecting generations.

Each individual in a peasant family worked not for his own benefit, but for the good of the entire family. Even if a family member worked at something other than farming, outside the family, away from home, he was still a member. And he was expected to contribute to the family.

The ordinary Chinese peasant could not read the writings of Confucius. Yet the five relationships Confucius had preached were embedded in his soul, deep within his tradition. They were passed on, generation to generation, by behavior and by stories, sayings, and fairy tales.

A peasant owning a whole acre of land might be considered well off in the village in which he lived, outside of which lay the fields all villagers worked. Upon his death the land, no matter how little, would be divided equally among his sons. It did not matter that there might be several sons, making each individual holding small. To begin with, leaving land to sons would insure that a father would be remembered after he was gone. As an ancestor, he would be honored. Secondly, each family hoped that the sons would work hard, save money, and buy more land.

Sons inherited, not daughters. Sons carried on the family name, and they might add more land to the family. Consequently sons were welcome additions to a family, daughters not so much so. A daughter simply grew up, got married, and went to live with her husband's family. "There are three things that are unfilial," wrote Mencius, a great Confucian

Opposite: Pottery figure of a woman, made during the Ch'in period and placed in a tomb as a servant for the spirits of the dead.

philosopher, "and to have no children is the greatest of these." To have no sons was nearly as bad.

A CHILD GROWS UP

Descriptions of traditional Chinese village life date from recent times. Yet they describe a way of life that remained practically unchanged for centuries. Wrote one observer, who grew up in a Chinese village, about childbirth:

The birth of a child, especially a boy, is tremendously important to a mother. When the young wife finds that she is pregnant, her thoughts, her interests, her activities, in short, her whole personality, begin to change. She thinks more and more of the coming of the child and asks her sisters-in-law to tell her what kind of child it will be. She is most interested in ascertaining its sex. She fears the birth pains, but she also looks forward to the honor which will be given to her as the mother of a child. Since she has been taught by her mother and mother-in-law that a child must be protected from evil spirits, certain foods, adverse emotions, and ill-omened words, she carefully avoids looking at abhorrent things, she becomes quiet, is often silent, and frequently falls into reverie. She watches herself carefully. When her husband comes upon her unexpectedly, her face reddens and she smiles at him with embarrassment. Occasionally her behavior may impress him, but usually he mocks her and belittles her seriousness. . . .

After the birth of the child, the mother is in constant attendance and generally wants very little assistance. She feeds him at her breast (later he will have liquid and soft foods) day and night. She changes his wet clothes and washes him frequently. She is the only one who attends the child in case of sickness, and it is she who worries most if the illness is serious. The young father shows no interest in his child; on the contrary, he is angry if it disturbs him by crying at night. Occasionally a father hates the very existence of his child. He will not touch it for any reason. He is embarrassed when a relative asks him about it, and to be seen actually holding the baby is a disgrace. He believes that he has helped in "making" the child, and that this in itself was shameful to him. He won't do anything to help because he believes that baby-tending is entirely a woman's job.

On the third day, the child was bathed and given its first garment, a little jacket made of a single piece of red cloth. He was then presented to his grandparents, and the family feasted on noodles made from flour, eggs, water, and powdered sesame seeds, and cooked without salt or sauce. This dish was thought to be good for the mother's milk and to speed her recovery. On this third day, too, the baby received a name. Boys were more prized than girls, and their names usually in some way referred to the family's prosperity and continuity. The name might be Hsi—joy, or Lo—happiness. It might be Kin—gold, or Kwei—highness. Or it might be Pao—precious, or Fa—prosperity. A girl was not expected to earn property or bring prosperity to the family. Her most important attributes were beauty and talent, which might result in a good marriage, and her name might well reflect these. It might be Ch'in—diligence, Cheng—chastity, or Sheng—thrift. Sometimes girls were given joking names like Hsia To—Little Too Many, or Hsiao Tsueh—Little Mistake.

When a child is three or four years old, he stays close to his mother most of the time.

Unless the grandmother is available to take care of him, he follows his mother around even when she is at work. One always sees a young wife with her child playing beside her as she washes her clothes on the river bank, grinds grain on a street corner, or works in the vegetable garden or on the threshing ground. By this time, however, she is usually pregnant again. When the second child is born, the mother will have to shift her attention from the first one. From this time on, the older child begins to sleep with his father instead of with his mother. The small family sleeps in the same bed, it is true, but it is a very broad one and the parents sleep at opposite ends of it. The baby sleeps beside the mother and the older child then moves to the father's side. When this change occurs, the father begins to dress the child, too. When the father is busy in the field, the boy is taken care of by his grandmother or by an older sibling. . . .

At the age of six or seven, a boy will either be sent to the village school, if the family is well-to-do, or be taken to the farm. If he goes to school, his duties at home will be light—sweeping the courtyard or carrying food to the field. During the harvesting seasons, he learns by trying to work within sight of his father. Sometimes he steals away from work or school, and enjoys for the first time the excitement of running wild with his playmates along the river bank or in the fields, free from the surveillance of an adult. If he does this too often, or if he injures himself or damages his clothing, he will certainly be punished by his father. He must be careful to avoid damaging any crops in his escapades or the punishment will be even more severe. In the absence of his father, his mother may punish him, but she will probably only threaten to do so. A mother usually punishes her son by scolding him or perhaps slapping his buttocks, if he is under ten years of age. When he is older she will seldom scold him directly and is even less likely to administer any physical punishment, which then becomes the sole duty of the father. Since a mother's heart is too soft to see her son beaten by an angry father, she often fails to report his misbehavior. Even a mother who believes in the necessity of discipline will tell only those deeds which she deems serious and then she tries to check the father lest the punishment be too severe. . . .

Although they frequently worked together in the field, father and sons were not close. The father always maintained dignity, joking little with his sons. He did not often unbend, expecting his sons always to obey and respect him. A son was much freer and more open with his mother. Between them, bonds of love and affection were close and freely expressed.

Most Chinese gained no schooling whatsoever. No one knows the precise illiteracy rate in traditional China, but it may have been as high as 90 percent. Girls did not attend school at all. Those relatively few boys who were to go usually entered at age seven.

The village school, though it had been built by the P'an clan and was mainly supported by them, was attended by boys from the entire village. . . .

The villagers regarded education as a means by which a family could raise its position. Children were taught to read names, to understand the content of land deeds, and to recognize the different kinds of paper money orders so that they would not be cheated in business transactions. The sons not needed for farm work were trained for a career, for business or a trade. Calligraphy [writing], account keeping, the use of the abacus, and the learning of the terms for farm products, farm implements, domestic utensils and manufactured commodities also held an important place in the curriculum, and there were some who regarded the school as the place where one learned good manners and absorbed the teachings of the ancient worthies. . . .

The students were sent to school before the sun was up each morning, about an hour before the teacher arrived. Each boy was expected to use this time in reading his assignment at the top of his voice and to memorize what he was reading. When the teacher appeared, another hour was spent in reviewing the textbooks. Then the boys were called up to recite one by one. Each boy, as his turn came, placed his books on the teacher's desk, turned his back, and recited all or parts of his assignment. All of this took place before breakfast. Both pupils and teachers went home to eat. When they returned from the morning meal, they practiced calligraphy and tried their skill at filling in couplets and composing poems. Occasionally there were lectures on good manners and on the ethical doctrines of Confucius. The teacher gave out the new assignments to each pupil individually, as there was no class system. . . .

In summer the school day ended around eight o'clock, when supper was served. In the winter, however, when supper was served much earlier, it was followed by another two-hour period of school. These evening sessions were usually spent in reading advanced textbooks or in writing short essays and poems. The local people regarded these winter evening classes as the most important part of the school term. Those parents who wanted their boys to prepare for the Imperial Examinations made sure that their sons did their best in the evenings. There was a common saying that any degree won from the Examination was the result of a great deal of oil and fire. . . .

Four years altogether were spent on schooling, and the curriculum was heavily weighted in favor of history and reading and reciting examples of ancient wisdom, along with calligraphy. Unless a boy was to prepare for the official examinations, his schooling ended at age ten or eleven. Those who did not go on to secondary school—the great majority—learned farming or a trade.

MARRIAGE

Regardless of his education or lack of it, for a young Chinese man marriage marked the entrance to adulthood. A single man of twenty-five was still looked upon as a boy; his parents were still responsible for his behavior. A married male of twenty was a man. Sometimes parents married a boy of fifteen to an older woman; such a youth too was considered to have become adult. The married young man

may not feel any change in himself, but the parents and the villagers have new expectations with regard to him. He no longer works for himself but for the economy of the family as a whole. His parents and other members of the family are ready to give him "face" before others, but his failures and weaknesses will not be easily excused as they were before his marriage. He now has the status of a married man: the villagers no longer address him by his "small name," and he may now represent his family at public affairs, if he is invited to do so. When the elders of a family say to a young man: "You are already more than twenty years old; it is time for you to marry and establish a career," the words are not spoken carelessly and the young man knows it is a warning. The injunctions as to marriage and career always occur together, for marriage is considered as primary to a career of any sort.

Girls, though loved, were of no benefit to a family. They would marry and leave to live with their husbands' families. Boys, however, would not only continue the family line, but, when married, would bring another working member into the family, one welcomed by an over-burdened mother.

Marriages are arranged by the parents, more specifically by the mother. When a family has a boy of fifteen or so, the matchmaking woman, a female relative or a friend of the parents, inquires if the boy is engaged. The mother is usually glad to answer, for if the boy is engaged she is proud of it, and if he is not she will be anxious for the inquirer to help. Such an inquiry is often merely a prelude to conversation, but if the woman asks this intentionally and says that she knows of a girl, then the talk takes a serious turn and proposal is started. The matchmaker visits the other family and poses the same question. If she happens to be related to the family, the question is unnecessary and she may begin the talk right away. The girl's mother may have a different attitude. If the girl is still young, say twelve or thirteen years old, and her physical appearance is not bad, and if the description of the boy's family is not particularly appealing, the mother may say to the matchmaker: "Thanks for your concern for us, but I feel that our little maid is not in a hurry. Let us leave the matter for the time being." This means that the offer has been refused. If, however, the girl is already twenty years old, and the mother realizes that she has no reason for a standard which would exclude ordinary boys, then she would probably say: "By all means, please help us to make this match. Day and night her father and I worry about finding her a *p'o-chia* (a family to which a daughter will be married). After all, we cannot keep daughters at home forever, can we? If the boy is good-natured and the family has enough to eat, I would say the

match is perfect. Anyway, I shall talk this matter over with her father."

At this, the matchmaker informs the boy's family of the birth date of the girl. It is written on paper with eight characters defining the year, month, date, and hour of the birth, or it is memorized. To determine the girl's compatibility with the boy and the members of his family, the girl's mother does the same with the boy's eight characters. The boy's mother consults some old ladies in the neighborhood who know a system of calculation based on the eight characters. If there is no one in the neighborhood who can read the characters, a professional fortune teller is consulted. . . .

As to the selection of a girl for marriage, beauty was far down the list of desirable qualities. Physical health to insure good births, efficiency in domestic work, freedom from physical and mental defects, and an unblemished reputation were much more important than physical appearance.

With respect to selecting a boy, on the other hand, the economic status of his family was the most important thing. Whether he was handsome or not did not matter. How much land his family possessed was a much more crucial issue. Second came his personality. Parents sought to avoid mating a daughter with a male who was hot tempered, or who had a reputation for drinking or gambling.

Once both families were satisfied, the boy's parents sent a formal letter to the girl's requesting that an engagement be made. They also sent gifts—food, cloth for dresses, or even money, depending on how well off the groom-to-be's parents were. Supposedly the gifts were for the bride. In actual fact they were payment to the parents for the girl, a common practice in numerous cultures, in some referred to as bride-price. The practice is quite the opposite of the dowry which in some cultures a bride brings to her husband or his family.

There were cases in traditional China in which parents pledged infants to marry into another family, even to sons yet unborn. In some instances parents sold an infant daughter outright to another family, who raised her in anticipation of her marriage to a son.

Arrangements agreed upon, an engagement ceremony took place at the girl's house, where her parents entertained the boy's father, other relatives, and guests, though not the prospective groom himself. At this time the father had an opportunity to inspect the girl, and she tendered her respects. The wedding itself might not take place for from three to five years later, depending on the ages of the boy and girl. And ceremonies among the more well-to-do, to which the following description refers, were more elaborate than among the poor.

On the morning of the wedding day, the boy's family sends a decorated bridal chair born by four able-bodied men to the girl's home. The four carriers are either the boy's cousins or young men of the village. . . . When the chair arrives at the girl's home, the bride, who has been waiting for it, is immediately carried into the chair by one of her elder brothers or by an uncle, while the mother weeps and the father stands silent. The bride wears a formal wedding dress or bridal robe of red or deep pink and her face is covered with a piece of red satin. The bridal chair is closed with a curtain so that nobody can see her on the road. Two brothers, close cousins, or perhaps her uncle, accompany her. On the road, the bridal procession proceeds slowly so that the bride will not get seasick, and also so that the enormous and extravagant dowry [groom's gifts] can be seen and admired by the people in the villages on the way. Meanwhile, the groom, attired in formal wedding gown of blue and jacket of black, waits in the wedding room.

When the bride arrives at the bridegroom's front door, two elderly women

Stone rubbings, taken from carvings made during the T'ang period, show scenes of rural life. Most of the activities depicted here continued without much change for centuries.

come out to meet her, while the men take care of the dowry and welcome the guests who have accompanied the bride. The women's duty is to transport the small boxes in which the bride's toilet articles are contained from the bridal chair to the *hsi-fang* [bridal room], and then to take the bride to the place where the wedding ceremony will be performed. This is usually the front court of the home, if the weather is good. In the center of the court is set a table on which are offerings to the gods of Heaven and Earth—a pair of red candles and three sticks of incense. The bride and groom stand side by side in front of the table and pay homage to the gods. Then, facing each other, the bride bows to the bridegroom and he returns the gesture. After this, they are led into the house and to the hsi-fang, the bridegroom walking ahead of the bride. She is helped by the two elderly women because her head is still covered. Meanwhile, a square piece of sweet cake,

wrapped with red cloth, is given to her by a sister of the bridegroom. A saddle, supposed to represent an evil spirit trying to block the union of the two, is placed in her path. Passing over it means the obstacles are overcome, the success of the marriage is assured. In the house both the bride and groom make ritual homage to the ancestors. . . . In the hsi-fang, the bride is seated on a wooden bed, while the groom takes his place on the brick bed. He is asked to take the red cloth off the bride's head. This is a very important moment to both bride and groom because they are to see each other face to face for the first time. The bride is fed with food which has been brought with her from her home and this is shared by the groom and his parents. After this, the bride is led to pay her respects to her parents-in-law and the groom accompanies her. When they return to their own room both of them will sit on the brick bed and the formal dresses are taken off [and clothes changed].

The young members of the family and of the neighborhood can now come to see the bride and look at the dowry. The bride is expected to sit on the bed quietly without speaking. The bridegroom also sits there looking very much embarrassed.

The whole family is busy entertaining guests. The two people who have accompanied the bride are the most honored guests and are entertained by senior members of the clan or village leaders, or by the schoolteacher. The feast is the best that the family can afford. The presents given by the relatives before the wedding day are used to help the family prepare for this occasion. Friends who come on the wedding day or before also bring gifts of money, a piece of satin bearing words of blessing or congratulations on golden paper, or perhaps merely a pair of paper scrolls with lucky words written on them. Popular phrases for this purpose are, "Give birth to a son early"; "Marriage that will last a hundred years"; and the like.

Three things sanctioned a marriage in traditional China: the bridal chair that transported the bride, the parade from the bride's home, and the ritual homage to the gods and to the husband's ancestors. Marriage needed no formal contract or license; it was not registered with any government agency. The bridal parade, above all, put the public on notice that a marriage would take place and sealed it.

The parade of the bridal chair and the dowry is for the purpose of showing that the marriage is being properly performed and also to let people see the dowry. The homage to the gods of Heaven and Earth assures that the marriage has been sanctioned by gods and not merely by men. The ceremony performed before the table of ancestors is a way of informing them that the woman has been properly introduced into the family and that hereafter she is one of them. She will assume full responsibility toward the living members and the spirits of the dead. Thus a Chinese marriage is recognized first by the two parties, second, by the two families and their relatives, third, by the society in which the couple is living, fourth, by the divinities. It is not surprising that a broken marriage in rural China is rarely seen.

Marital unions were arranged by parents because marriage's chief objectives were to produce children and continue the family line ancestors had established, and at the same time to provide sons to insure old-age comfort and security. Its secondary purpose was to acquire a daughter-in-law as additional household help. Marriage was intended to expand the family and lend it additional security and protection. Consequently the desires, even the welfare, of the man and woman directly involved were of no importance. Individuals, in marriage and in other ways, were subordinated to the welfare and continuity of the group. To allow individual choice, or marriage based on romantic love, would simply open the door to uncertainty and possible blunder. All of this would threaten the well-being and solidarity of the family.

With respect to women, the system had severe shortcomings. A wife was, in the strict sense of the word, bought. No matter how loved, a daughter, especially in a peasant family, was basically an economic asset. Since upon marriage she left her household, she deprived her family of a unit of labor. The family expected compensation for that. Forsaking her own family, moving into her husband's house, a wife was considered by her new family basically as labor and a producer of children. In the male-dominated society that was traditional China women were completely subservient to men. A girl obeyed her father, a married woman her husband, a widow her son. Women enjoyed no legal rights. Divorce for a man was a simple matter of sending a wife back to her parents. The husband possessed the right to keep the children, if any. Divorce was no matter for a court of law or any other part of government. For a woman, particularly one of the peasant class, divorce remained next to impossible regardless of how cruel a husband and his family might be to her. For a widow to remarry was extremely difficult. According to custom a woman was married to one man only, regardless of how long she might survive him. And if a widow did manage remarriage, any children by her deceased husband by right belonged to his family, and she could take with her no property save personal belongings. Widows were to be virtuous. Thanks to these circumstances, the suicide rate among widows in traditional China was high.

REMEMBERING GODS
AND ANCESTORS

Gods and ancestors played important roles in marriage ceremonies, as they did in day-to-day rural life as well. A Chinese family may have been Buddhist or Taoist, or both. But it also attended to the old nature gods and to ancestors. This was especially true on New Year's, the greatest festival of the year, a religious as well as a secular celebration.

For the homeless, New Year's was a miserable time. It was solely an occasion for the family, a time when members of the family gathered to participate in ceremonies related to origins and future and to pay homage to ancestors. Non-family members consequently were not welcome, including intimate friends and even daughters-in-law. They had to seek out their own families or remain alone. Even the kitchen god was banished for a time. The celebration lasted about a month, and prior to

the New Year, the entire house was cleaned and any broken item carefully repaired. Food was prepared well in advance for the family, for offerings to ancestors, and for guests when time for New Year's visiting came.

Two days before New Year's Eve, doors were cleaned with water and scrubbed with sand. The next day a table was set against the north wall of the house and incense sticks, candles, and various articles of food were placed on it.

After the evening meal, the father and a young son went to the ancestral graveyard to invite the spirits home. Later, the family performed a ceremony at the front door to welcome the gods of wealth, heaven and earth, the kitchen god, and spirits of unknown dead relatives. Then the family went to bed.

Very early the next morning, at two o'clock, the family awoke and, putting on their best or new clothes, gathered at the ceremonial table. There they lighted incense sticks and candles and bowed toward objects considered reminders of ancestors. The ceremony ended with the lighting of lanterns. Then the father set off a string of firecrackers, a signal that the religious part of New Year's had ended and secular activities could commence.

Over the next several days there were ceremonies to honor ancestors, much visiting between families, and great feasting. The last of the New Year's food was eaten at the Lantern Festival, which fell on the fifteenth day of the New Year, concluding the New Year's celebration.

There were additional festivals throughout the year. One, Ch'ing Ming, coming at the beginning of the third month, celebrated the warming of the earth in north China. Another was the Harvest Festival, a joyous time during the eighth month—provided a good harvest appeared likely. But no celebration compared with New Year's. None stressed the importance of the family and the intermingling of land and family, living and dead, quite so much.

The Chinese tended to "humanize" their gods, and while they believed in the Supreme Ruler of Heaven, he was but one of many deities. Chinese viewed their gods as needing food and clothing, just as humans do, and as capable of anger or pleasure as humans are. Consequently, food was frequently offered to gods along with pleas for good crops or fortune or deliverance from disaster. Droughts, floods, and typhoons were considered indications of gods' wrath and their demand for appeasement. Every Chinese village contained a variety of temples to gods, and the Chinese annually celebrated the "birthdays" of the Dragon God, the God of Agriculture, and others, including Buddha.

WHEN DEATH CAME

When death claimed a family member, the Chinese turned to Buddhism as well as the old religions for ceremony and for solace. The Chinese believed that the soul, upon the body's death, was subject to reward or punishment, or both, determined by the courts of ten judges who reviewed a soul's merits and demerits after its departure from earth. A soul might be punished, then sent off for further misery in one or all of the eighteen or more hells. Most souls eventually underwent reincarnation. Those who had led particularly bad lives were condemned to endless reincarnation as beggars, disease-ridden persons, or animals to be hunted and killed. A soul possessing much merit, on the other hand, was met at the spirit world by a reception committee playing music and bearing food. After lavish entertainment the soul might be offered appointment as a local god on earth or, if especially deserving, perhaps be sent to eternal happiness in the Western Paradise, a Buddhist heaven.

Donning white garments and pasting white paper on doors and windows, the survivors mourned their loss. Wailing began the moment the person drew his final breath and continued until burial. After the body was placed in the coffin, in the house, food offerings were set before it and incense was burned.

The funeral procession, if that of a large family, was immense, and wailing was especially sad and loud. A Buddhist priest recited prayers and the procession set off slowly, accompanied by boys bearing banners on which were written characters praising the deceased. Mourners carried a paper house and other paper articles. And, if the family could afford it, there was a brass band. Finally, at the cemetery, the coffin was lowered into the ground as each mourner dropped a handful of earth on it. If the deceased was a parent, he now had become an ancestor, to be remembered always. And to prevent forgetting, throughout the year there were numerous ceremonies and celebrations, such as New Year's, to bring ancestors vividly to mind.

There was in China no clear-cut line between religion and philosophy, between Buddhism, the nature gods, Taoism, and Confucianism. Religion centered on the family, and this involved ancestors and what was known as their worship.

Yet no one should think of ancestor worship in terms of churches, prayers, the deification of individuals, and so on. A better term is veneration, and the idea of honoring ancestors rested on three assumptions.

One assumption was that an individual owed his fortune or misfortune to ancestors. A beggar was a beggar due to laziness. Yet had his ancestors accumulated more merit, they might have had a more honorable descendant. A person's achievement, likewise, was evidence of ancestors' moral worth and standing.

Secondly, all departed ancestors, the Chinese believed, possessed the same needs as their descendants still on earth. Consequently the living must offer ancestors food as well as models of furniture, clothing, animals, and other items they required. If offerings were not made, departed spirits would turn into vagabonds, and in the eyes of the community those descendants would appear most unfilial.

Finally, according to Chinese belief, ancestors could and did assist descendants in the same way the living aided each other. Confucian principles demanded mutual aid and respect among those on earth. And those principles also referred to ancestors who, as the following story shows, could help the living.

An imperial examiner was in his studio reading the examination papers of candidates for the great honors. As he reviewed them, he put the papers in two piles—those which he marked "consider again" and those which he decided to "flunk outright." Beginning his perusal of the "consider again" pile, he picked up one which he was sure he had already discarded into the other group. He discarded it a second time. But a few moments later he came upon it once more in the "consider again" stack. Just when the annoyed examiner was about to discard it for the third time, a spirit appeared before him. They conversed, and the spirit convinced him that this particular paper, written by one of the spirit's great-grandchildren, deserved to be reconsidered. The examiner did so and passed the candidate.

The Chinese believed the world of spirits to be identical to life on earth. Save that the dead were no longer present, there was no difference between the spirits and the living. The world of the spirits and that of the living was not sharply and clearly divided. Family, like time, was circular and continuous.

For the peasant family, weddings, births, funerals, and festivals were special events. Day to day, there was nearly always work to do, as they performed the task of wrenching a living from the soil.

In southern China, which enjoyed a warm climate, rice was the important grain crop, and the average peasant's holding totalled no more than an acre. Rice shoots were started on small plots, then transplanted by hand, laboriously, to flooded paddies. Once the rice ripened, the paddies were drained and the grain was harvested and threshed, by hand. Usually peasants in southern China grew two crops of rice a year. In addition, they raised tea plants, and mulberry bushes to produce food for silkworms, which spun fibers from which thread was made for cloth. Southern China was also a land of citrus fruits, bananas, and other subtropical and tropical fruits.

North China, where Chinese civilization began, endured a much harsher climate, with cold, snowy winters and frequently terribly hot summers. Here individual peasant holdings tended to be a trifle larger than those in the south, and here winter wheat and millet were the grain crops. Peasants also frequently planted sweet potatoes, peanuts, and soybeans in tiny gardens. They kept a few animals, such as oxen for plowing, and pigs, mainly for the fertilizer they produced, not for food.

August was the month for plowing winter wheat land, September the month for planting. Then peasants could do nothing but wait, hoping for a good snow cover which would mean a good wheat harvest the following June.

The Chinese peasant's life was most precarious, threatened always by drought, flood, taxes, forced labor on government projects, and army service.

THE PLIGHT OF THE PEASANT

To the ordinary peasant, that government which taxed and now and then demanded sons and labor was far away. It had little meaning for him, and no direct influence. If the peasant thought of the central government at all, it was in terms of "they" or "them," not "we" or "us." Sometimes the government did something for a person. It might, for example, from time to time provide grain for the people during a time of famine. More often, it did something to a person—deprived him of a portion of his crop for taxes, a son for the army, or time from his fields to help build a dike or road. But the peasant himself was not a part of the government; most of the time government to him simply was a burden. Followers of both Lao Tzu and Confucius agreed that a ruler's chief virtue should be humility toward the people. Both groups subscribed to the thought behind this song from the ancient *Book of History*:

The people should be cherished,
And should not be downtrodden.
The people are the root of a country,
And, if the root is firm, the country will be
    tranquil.

Practice, however, did not always jibe with philosophy.

To the ordinary peasant, government was a local thing, something with which he had contact at least once a year when tax payments fell due. Villages and towns were not governed according to law in the sense of a body of legislation for reference in settling disputes or determining and dealing with crime. They were governed in accord with custom. Custom possessed all the force of written law—even more—for centuries of usage had ingrained it in the people. They accepted it without question. Custom governed ordinary behavior in China and custom determined how the community would handle deviant behavior on the part of any member. Elders governed on the local level, chosen by other elders or self-appointed. They determined taxes, judged and decided disputes, and meted out punishment when appropriate. In determining whether an offense had been committed, how serious it was, and what the punishment should be, a person's social position, his background, his past record, his motivation, and other aspects of the situation all received consideration.

Control of village affairs rested in the hands of the gentry. Gentry were landowners as a

Opposite: Pottery model of the courtyard of a house with men and animals. These objects were placed in a tomb for the use of the spirits of the dead, probably during the Sung Dynasty.

This scene, painted by Ch'en Hung-shou in 1650, shows the poet T'ao Ch'ien being carried to a friend's house by his servants.

rule, but they were also members of the scholar-literati. They had passed at least the district examinations, yet held no official government position. Below the district level in traditional China, there was no official government administration. This role was filled by the gentry. Its members either occupied the offices of village head, tax collector, and the like, or, being influential, controlled the persons who did hold them.

Throughout the centuries the gentry on the village level served vital functions. As the educated and the landowning, they performed necessary governmental tasks. They acted as a buffer between the village and the district government, during times of stress trying to get taxes lowered, working to obtain money for roads and for flood control. Frequently gentry supported local candidates for the official examinations. In the absence of banks of any kind on the local level, the gentry of necessity,

if for no other reason, became bankers.

Many peasants were landowners too. Some, by village standards, were rich. But peasants, rich or poor, labored in the fields. Gentry did not. As members of the scholar-literati they grew long fingernails and wore robes as a symbol of disdain and lack of need for physical labor. Gentry, some living in towns, others in villages, earned income in cash or crops by renting land. They gained even more from lending money, frequently at exceedingly high interest rates. Gentry were the town and village upper class, and they ruled the traditional Chinese countryside with a firm, and in too many cases a cruel, greedy, or thoughtless hand. To understand the position of the gentry and its relationship to the peasantry is to gain one inkling of why revolution finally came to China and how it was that revolution should be Communist-led and, eventually, successful.

CHANGCHUANG

The village of Changchuang, brush strokes for which in the written language can be translated Long Bow, lies in the southeast portion of Shansi province in north China, on high plateau country north of the Yellow River, four hundred miles southwest of Peking. A New Zealander, William Hinton, became acquainted with Long Bow in the late 1940s when the village, like all China, was undergoing transition from tradition to modernity.

Life and conditions that had persisted in Long Bow may not have been typical, even of north China which is considerably different from the warmer, more humid south. Yet millions of Chinese peasants who must have led at least a somewhat similar life rose up under the leadership of Mao Tse-tung and worked a revolution. One might guess that they had reasons, possibly similar to those which over the centuries generated in the breasts of Changchuang residents.

"For how many centuries prior to [my arrival] this village had endured in this place almost without change I do not know," wrote Hinton.

Certainly for hundreds of years, any tired traveler who paused to rest at the crest of the hill and looked out over the flat land to the north saw substantially the same sight —a complex of adobe walls under a canopy of trees set in the middle of a large expanse of fields. These fields were barren, brown and desolate in winter, while in summer they were green, yellow, and clothed with diverse crops.

To look down on this valley in January was to look upon a world of frozen immobility. Through most of each day not even a wisp of smoke could be seen curling up from the squat mud chimneys that poked above the gently sloping roofs marking the settlement; the rich, who kept their fires burning day and night, burned a coal and earth mixture that gave off no smoke, and the poor, who burned roots, straw, and wild dry grasses, lit their fires only at mealtime, and then only long enough to boil a few handfuls of millet.

In the depths of winter the temperature often went below zero. Rich and poor alike stayed indoors. Only on the main north-south road could any sign of human activity be seen. This was the route taken by the carters who hauled freight out of the mountains regardless of weather.

With the coming of warm weather this all but lifeless scene was transformed. From the first cock-crow in the semi-darkness before dawn until the red sun went down behind the western mountains at night, peasants by the hundreds came and went on the land, plowing, hauling manure, planting, harvesting. There were always so many people in the fields that they could talk to one another as they worked without leaving their own plots.

THE PEOPLE AND THE LAND

The population of the village varied drastically in size. A poor crop year could easily cut the number of residents in half, a part of the poor dying in the huts where they lived and the rest fleeing to other regions in a desperate gamble for survival. By and large, however, the thousand acres of land that encircled the village could support between 200 and 300 families, and no sooner did famine on the Shangtang plateau cut down the number of Long Bow people and drive them to other places than famine in other parts of North China drove new people to the plateau to settle in their place....

Counting noses among the 200-odd families one could ordinarily tally up about a thousand persons altogether. This meant that on the average there was one acre of land for every man, woman, and child. The crops from this one acre, in a good year, were ample for the support of a single person, considering the very low standard of living that prevailed. But the poor who rented land or worked out as hired laborers got less than half the crops they tilled, while the rich got the surplus from many acres. That is why some were able to build enormous underground tombs marked for eternity, or so they thought, with stone tortoises bearing obelisks inscribed with the family name, while others when they died were thrown into a hole in the ground with only a reed mat wrapped around them and a few shovelfuls of earth to mark the place.

Graves large and small dotted the land around Long Bow. As if this were not enough obstruction to tillage, the fields were divided into countless narrow strips and plots, each one owned by a different family. Even on the level there were few fields larger than half an acre, while on the hill, where the land was terraced, there were strips only a few yards wide that ran in great S curves around the slopes, and small triangles at the top end of gullies that contained but a few square yards of ground. Land was so valuable in the Shangtang that the peasants found it necessary to build stone walls as high as 15 feet to hold back a few feet of earth and make it level. Where the hills were too steep to terrace, they plowed anyway and cropped the ground for a year or two until the soil washed away completely. In the mountains to the east of Long Bow village men plowed hillsides so steep that an extra person was needed to stand on the slope above and keep tension on a rope tied around the ox lest he slip and roll away.

The crops grew only on what was put into the soil each year; hence manure was the foundation of the whole economy. The chief source of supply was the family privy, and this became, in a sense, the center of the household.

Animal manure, together with any straw, stalks, or other waste matter, was composted in the yard. So highly was it valued that old people and children constantly combed the roads and cart tracks for droppings which they scooped up and carried home in baskets. This need to conserve every kind of waste and return it to the land was responsible for the tidy appearance of the streets and courtyards even though the walls were crumbling and the roofs falling in. Nothing, absolutely nothing, was left lying around. Even the dust of the street was swept up and thrown on the compost heap or into the privy, for village dust was more fertile, by far, than the soil in the fields.

The clothes that people wore and the food that they ate were all products of the village land. Even the gentry, who possessed for festive occasions silks and satins imported from the South, donned for everyday wear the same homespun cottons that served to clothe their servants and their tenants. Though styles did evolve over the centuries, the basic workday clothing changed little. In summer everyone wore thin jackets and pants of natural cotton bleached white or dyed blue or black with indigo. Long Bow women liked to wear white jackets and black pants, but this was by no means universal.

In cold weather everyone wore clothes padded with cotton. . . . Each day that one survived was a day to be thankful for and so, throughout the region, in fat years and in lean, the common greeting came to be not "Hello" or "How are you?" but a simple, heartfelt "Have you eaten?"

GENTRY RULE

In Long Bow, as landowners and landlords, as moneylenders and as the government, the gentry ruled, reinforced with confidence bred from centuries of control.

This confidence of the gentry was based on the stability of the land system and the culture it engendered—a system and a culture that had survived and often flourished since before the time of Christ. Under this system . . . a typical community was made up of a small number of landlords and rich peasants and a large number of hired laborers, poor peasants, and middle peasants. The landlords and rich peasants, who made up less than 10 percent of the rural population, owned from 70 to 80 percent of the land, most of the draft animals, and the bulk of the carts and implements. The hired laborers, the poor peasants, and the middle peasants, who made up more than 90 percent of the population, held less than 30 percent of the land, only a few draft animals, and a scattering of implements and carts— a condition which placed them perennially at the mercy of the more well-to-do and condemned them to a life of veritable serfdom. . . .

Long Bow's richest family, the seven-member household of the landlord Sheng Ching-ho, tapped every [possible] income source. Sheng Ching-ho was a healthy, able-bodied man, but he never engaged in any form of manual labor. He did not have to. His income was many times that of the most prosperous middle-peasant family. He cultivated long fingernails, wore a long gown that made manual work impossible, and considered it beneath his dignity even to lift his bag onto his cart when he went on a trip.

The heart of Ching-ho's "empire" consisted of 23 acres of fertile land. . . . To work these acres he hired two year-round laborers, plus extra hands at harvest time. In livestock, the second most important category of rural wealth, he owned two draft animals, a flock of sheep, and several hogs. He employed two boys full-time to look after the sheep. His industrial enterprise was a small distillery where *paikar* was made from grain. The wine cost about 20 cents a catty [1.1 pounds] to make and sold for about 30 cents a catty. When in full production this distillery turned out over 100 catties a day. In this plant Ching-ho employed two men for about seven months every year. The distiller's grains left over from the process were fed to fattening hogs.

The income from these enterprises was fairly large and since the family lived very frugally, Sheng Ching-ho had a yearly surplus. Some of this surplus he converted into silver coin which he buried in the back part of his courtyard. Another part he invested in a distillery owned by another landlord, Fan Pu-tzu. The rest he loaned out to peasants in desperate need and, by charging exhorbitant interest rates (up to 50 percent a month), often doubled or tripled his principal in one season. Those who were unable to pay lost their land to him. If they had no land, they lost their livestock, their carts, their implements. This loan business was actually run by his wife, a woman with a very sharp business head who kept careful track of every copper coin.

With his wife in command of the loans, Ching-ho himself had plenty of time for such equally lucrative operations as managing the affairs of the Pei Lao Shih or North Temple Society, a charitable organization set up to help support the village school, lend money to members in distress, give insurance-type benefits, and placate the gods.

As a fertility and good luck offering to the gods, each member of the North Temple Society had to pay annually a certain amount of grain per acre. All this grain went to Ching-ho's home and eventually found its way to his distillery. No accounting for this wealth was ever made to the people. . . .

MANY MEANS OF INCOME

Ching-ho also headed the K'ung Tzu Tao —Confucian Association—which drew members from thirty villages altogether. The cost of periodic banquets Ching-ho staged for the Association was usually lower than the amounts he collected from members to pay for them. Ching-ho also managed spirit talking, or conversations with the dead, which the Association arranged for those who desired them. This netted him fees of course.

For many years Sheng Ching-ho served as village head under the governor of Shensi province. There was no salary attached, but as village head Ching-ho received invitations to holiday feasts, took favors in return for settling disputes over land ownership and the like, and he could collect graft on tax payments and on public works projects. As for taxes, if the county magistrate asked for two bushels of grain per family, as likely as not Ching-ho would demand five per family and keep three. And he collected taxes even if peasants had to sell their children to pay for them. Of course he had to split his take with various tax and other officials, but on the whole Ching-ho did well.

Ching-ho overlooked no opportunity to use his wealth to breed further wealth.

. . . Han-sheng was an old man who owned half an acre of very good land just to the east of the village. In a crisis he once borrowed $13 from Sheng Ching-ho. Three years later the principal plus interest amounted to a very large sum. Though Han-sheng paid off some of it, he couldn't pay it all. Ching-ho then seized the half-acre and the summer harvest that had just been reaped on it. Because he did not want the millet he plowed it under and planted wheat in the fall. Han-sheng was left with nothing.

The middle peasant Shih Szu-har borrowed $125 from the North Temple Society managed by Ching-ho. Two years later, when Szu-har was unable to pay, he lost his land—all six acres, his eleven-section house, his donkey, and his cart. The whole family, including very young children, were driven outside to live in the open. Luckily Szu-har had both loyal friends and skill as a carpenter. He found shelter and work and was able to save his family from starvation. . . .

Rich peasants could be as rapacious as some gentry. In Long Bow Kuo Ch'ung-wang and his brother Fu-wang, who owned twenty-two acres of land, were known as the meanest employers in the whole village. They too insisted on prompt rent and loan payments regardless of circumstances and did not hesitate to wipe out poor peasants who could not comply.

Unquestionably there were gentry whose behavior was on a higher level than that of Long Bow's gentry. But even under the best of gentry the Chinese peasant's life was hard. And generally his situation worsened beginning in the 1920s when the central government—a dictatorship of the Kuomintang, or Nationalist Party, led by Chiang Kai-shek—grew increasingly oppressive and corrupt.

In Long Bow, as undoubtedly in many other villages, everyone—gentry and peasants, poor and rich alike—were to some extent victims of circumstances, caught in a seamless web. There was no commerce or industry in Long Bow, nothing to invest in save land and, on the whole, the land was poor. Returns from it for anyone, whether worker or simply investor, were exceedingly small. The land could have been made more productive with irrigation, but the necessary technology was lacking. Better seeds and more fertilizer might have helped, but there was no guarantee of success and increased yields might well have been lost to taxes. Poor peasants—the majority of the Chinese population—were poor risks, and those without land at all the poorest. Even a distillery such as Ching-ho's found many willing to drink its product, but relatively few who could get up the price to pay for it. And peasants borrowed, through necessity, for consumption, not for production. Loans usually went to pay for weddings, funerals, and food needed to tide a family over until the next harvest. The money was in no sense squandered, but it did not go to improve the land or farm implements, to increase production—in the long run, perhaps, to make life better.

YEARS OF ENDURANCE

Despite the iron grip of circumstances which affected everyone, many gentry could still be faulted for worsening an already bad situation. They enjoyed warm clothes, a secure, tight roof over their heads, bedclothes to keep them comfortable in winter, ample fuel for their fires, and a varied diet at their tables. They were the envy of the peasants and one must wonder why peasants endured their lot with such apparent patience. There were at least four reasons.

Because of Confucian teaching and tradition, for one thing. Peasants believed in the private ownership of property as deeply as anyone else. Each wanted to own land and acquire more. Land was China, and China, land. Those who owned land enjoyed power, for everyone depended on land for survival. But according to Confucian teaching, success in the quest for land, as success in anything else, was regarded as a reward for virtuous living, right Confucian thinking, and proper conduct. A poor peasant's lot could be blamed on his lack of virtue.

Religion had something to do with it too. **53** The average Chinese believed in luck and good fortune, bestowed by the spirits. The spirits had smiled on the gentry, but on few peasants. In addition, Buddhism, which attracted many Chinese, emphasized a passive acceptance of one's fate, be it good or poor.

Thirdly, and especially important, the gentry controlled local government and the means to enforce their will. Justice that the local government administered was individualistic, and for a peasant it could often be discouraging. It was not uncommon for a member of the gentry to administer what he considered justice alone and informally. Frequently a person caught stealing food was flogged or beaten on the spot, regardless of how sharply hunger drove him or whether he was a man or young boy. Death from internal injuries sometimes resulted.

Finally, and also important, peasants possessed no political cohesion. They tended to think and behave as individuals, their horizons no wider than the individual family. Peasants were bound by the necessity of planting, growing, and harvesting, without which they themselves could not survive. They lacked arms and experience with them, lacked leadership and the long-range vision necessary for struggle against oppression. They were, as William Hinton put it, "in the position of a man trying to survey the sky while imprisoned at the bottom of a well."

Not that peasants did not from time to time rise up. Throughout the centuries, more than a thousand peasant rebellions were recorded, and no one knows how many escaped history's notice. The Yellow Turban Rebellion which signalled the beginning of the end of the Han Dynasty was but one of many. Most rebellions were unorganized, however; they were spontaneous, and lacked power to sustain themselves. Most were desperate moves by peasants at the end of endurance, frequently following a series of natural disasters such as epidemic, flood, drought, and famine.

器用聚鋼條及浸水黑石沙　凡玉體重極即宜用此圖內

所畫之器以開之　　至若玉重二三十斤則以天秤吊

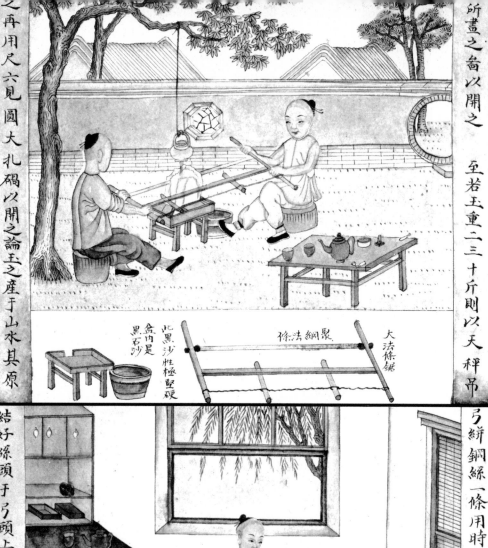

此黑石沙性極堅硬

為內是黑石沙

徐法鋼鋸

大法條鋸

之再用尺六見圓大扎碢以開之論玉之產于山水其原

體脊有石皮今欲用其玉必先其去皮若剝菓皮而取

其仁也故云開玉此攻玉第一工也

凡玉匕宜作透花者先以鋼鑽將玉匕鑽透圓孔後以

弓絣鋼絲一條用時則解鋼絲一頭隨將絲頭穿過玉孔仍

結好絲頭于弓頭上然後用浸水沙順花樣以搜之如木

作彎鋸搜花一樣　圖內棹上有豎木棹拿子或

橫木棹拿以穩住玉器

絲鋼

弓搜

式圖解絲鋼手背弓

系鋼

整木棹拿

橫木棹拿

Villages clustered around market towns. There people could exchange goods produced in their local areas, such as vegetables and grain, for such items as salt, iron tools, and different kinds of fruits. Merchants supplied these commodities and saw to it that they were transported from their place of origin to the market towns.

There was considerable trade within China, and between Chinese and people of other countries. Many merchant families grew rich from trade, yet in China merchants as a group were not honored or respected. In public esteem they ranked below gentry and peasants who owned and farmed the land, and they were far below the scholar-literati.

"The gentleman cherishes virtue," Confucius said. "The inferior man cherishes possessions. The gentleman understands what is right. The inferior man understands what is profitable." A scholar-official was considered a virtuous man. Even a landlord might be. A merchant, never.

Merchants were not productive. They did not grow food, as peasants did. They did not produce tools and other useful items as craftsmen did, nor govern, as the scholar-literati did. Merchants simply lived off the labor of others, buying and selling what other people produced, or, as in the case of salt, what nature itself supplied. Merchants may have been necessary, but they were not respected. From the Confucian point of view they were simply among those who existed to support the wise and learned men who governed. Land was the only wealth esteemed in traditional China. Money wealth was uncertain, transient, and generally considered to be ill-gotten.

Chinese governments at an early time established firm control over trade and the exchange of certain necessities of life. The government, for example, regulated the sale of salt as well as iron production. Later, such items as tea and silk were added to the list. By regulating trade closely, government officials gained from it. Conse-

Opposite: Craftsmen sawing crude jade into pieces and carving the jade. These sketches from a book published around 1900 illustrate techniques jade workers had mastered centuries earlier.   55

quently it was not in their interest to allow free trade entirely, or to allow merchants to become important and influential in their own right.

From time to time the Chinese government granted a group of merchants a monopoly on certain items, giving only one group the right to deal in a commodity such as salt. In exchange, monopolists paid the government for the privilege and collected taxes on salt for the government.

During the 1700s a group of merchants called the Yang Chou, named after the town in which they had headquarters, held the salt monopoly. They grew exceedingly rich, becoming perhaps the richest merchants of the time in all of China. And they spent their money freely, in such ways as to attract considerable attention to themselves and prove their wealth.

The Yang Chou merchants sponsored lavish wedding feasts, held elaborate funerals, and gave great dinner parties at which many servants served meals of countless courses. One Yang Chou merchant fancied horses, raising them by the hundreds. Another favored orchids, constantly replenishing huge displays of them all about his house. Still another merchant, wishing to be really outstanding, sought to spend $10,000 in a single day. Following a friend's suggestion, he bought thin gold foil and, from a hilltop, scattered the foil far and wide, allowing the wind to waft delicate strands of gold here and there to melt against trees and grass below. This exhibition was difficult to top, but other Yang Chou merchants tried.

Some merchants, including those who dealt in salt, spent their money more wisely. Some helped poor scholars, others hired scholars to develop libraries. Others nurtured beautiful flower gardens in their courtyards. Still others supported bright sons who studied hard and became scholar-literati, thus removing themselves from the despised merchant class.

On the other side of the world, in Europe, a merchant class developed too. There, however, a merchant was not looked down upon by government officials or by anyone. On the contrary, a wealthy merchant was a most honored and respected man. In Europe, on the whole, money wealth was considered as valuable and important as wealth in land, among some people even more so.

The two views of the worth of merchants—Chinese and European—would clash. So would the Chinese and European views on the value of science and technology. And so would the ideas about which area, China or Europe, really was the center of the universe.

A wealthy man, at ease in his luxurious home, was painted by Liu Kuan-Tao in the early fourteenth century.

Among the first Europeans to visit China, or Cathay as it was then called, and write about what he had experienced was Marco Polo. With his father and his uncle, traveling overland and by sea from Venice, in Italy, Polo reached China in the 1270s. And there he remained for twenty years, serving the emperor as a government official.

China was not under Chinese rule at the time Polo lived there. It had been conquered by the Mongols, fierce nomads from the north. Sweeping out of central Asia in the thirteenth century astride shaggy ponies, Mongol warriors had overrun much of China and extended their influence as far west as Hungary in central Europe, raping, pillaging, and destroying as they went. Mongols ruled the greatest empire the world had ever known and in China they established the Yüan Dynasty, governing mainly through Chinese officials. Not until 1368, with the establishment of the Chinese Ming Dynasty, was Mongol control of China eliminated.

Marco Polo wrote a book about his experiences in China, and a few other Italian traders followed him there. A number of Christian missionaries as well as traders from other parts of Europe visited China too during the time of Mongol rule.

As the Ming period began, it appeared that China might continue and even expand its contacts and trade with other lands. In the early 1400s, the Ming emperor sent several fleets of great ships out into the Indian Ocean, the first expedition consisting of sixty-two vessels and thousands of men. Other expeditions ranged as far west as the Red Sea and Africa, one ship returning from Africa with a live giraffe which was presented to the emperor.

But just as suddenly as these great sailing expeditions had begun, they stopped. No such event occurred again in Chinese history. Instead of expanding contacts, the Chinese gradually withdrew from the world, wishing to have little or nothing to do with foreigners.

VOYAGES OF DISCOVERY AND EXPLORATION

Foreigners, however, were of another mind. Europeans had learned about the compass, invented in China centuries before, and they mastered its use on sailing ships sturdy enough to withstand ocean storms. Europeans had also learned about gunpowder and how to manufacture it. Firecrackers, however, did not interest them. Europeans quickly discovered how gunpowder

Opposite: This fourteenth century scroll portrays a festival at a summer palace.

could be used as an explosive to fire iron balls from cannons, which could be mounted on ships. Vessels bearing cannons proved to be powerful instruments of war and trade.

Christopher Columbus, an Italian like Marco Polo, read Polo's book on China and from it drew inspiration to lay great plans to sail west from Europe to reach that fabled land. This led, in 1492, to Columbus' arrival in the Americas after a few weeks' voyage across the Atlantic Ocean.

In the meantime, sea captains from Portugal, next door to Spain, had been pushing ever southward on the Atlantic, seeking to find the southernmost point of Africa and round it into the Indian Ocean. Visions of obtaining

Porcelain Ming vase.

spices, gold, silks, and precious jewels in India and on islands to the southeast known as the Indies, spurred on the Portuguese. And in 1488 Bartholomeu Díaz reached the Cape of Good Hope, the southern tip of Africa. Ten years later Vasco da Gama, following Díaz' route, sailed on to reach Calcutta, India with four ships. The Portuguese found Indians interested in trade and from India and the Indies Portuguese merchants reaped great wealth.

Moving on to China later, seeking to expand their trade, the Portuguese found a different situation. The Chinese government had no interest in trade with Europeans. Finally, though, in 1517, the government allowed two Portuguese traders to operate in Canton, in the south, but in that city only. Unsatisfied, the Portuguese demanded more rights and privileges and at last, weary of the bearded, white-skinned foreigners, the Ming government ordered them to leave the country. It allowed no more Portuguese in China for the next twenty years.

CONTRASTING CULTURES

Portuguese, like other Europeans, tended to divide the people of the world into whites and other colors and into Christians and followers of "pagan" religions. In addition, to them western Europe was the center of the world. From their point of view, white Christian Europeans were superior, all other peoples of the world inferior, barbarous, and backward. Europeans considered it their duty to "civilize" other peoples, to subdue pagan religions and Christianize the world. Trade, highly profitable to merchants, was the avenue toward the accomplishment of European goals.

The Chinese possessed a slightly different point of view. They nursed no racial or religious prejudices, as Europeans did, but they did have a high regard for their own culture. High Chinese civilization had flourished at a time when Europeans were scarcely out of the caveman stage. The Chinese, considering their land the center of the universe, could not conceive of a civilization that came even close to equalling their own. The Chinese were civilized, all other peoples barbarians. Until about the time of Christ, the Chinese knew little or nothing about civilizations that existed in India and under the Romans in the Mediterranean area. Even after that, although there was some trade in such goods as silks and spices between China and other areas, Chinese information about the rest of the world through the centuries remained sketchy. Rulers of lands under Chinese control, such as Assam, now a state in India, Annam, now Vietnam, and Korea were expected to recognize their inferiority and pay annual tribute to the emperor, the Son of Heaven on the Dragon Throne. And when representatives appeared at the court with tribute, they were required first to kow-tow—kneel three times, then stretch themselves out facedown nine times before the emperor. The Chinese expected Europeans to pay tribute and to kow-tow too. Europeans, in the Chinese view, were no less inferior than any other people.

Here the Chinese may have had a point. During Marco Polo's time, for example, no European country could boast of broad highways and canals and beautiful cities as China could. European cities were garbage-strewn, smelly, and rat-infested. European nobles lived in castles, dark, damp, stone buildings surrounded by ditches called moats, which were filled with water, smelly, and breeding grounds for mosquitoes. Castle windows were simply narrow slits between the stones. Floors were strewn with greasy straw which was not often changed, and in the dining room the straw was mixed with bones and other garbage tossed from the table. Lords and ladies seldom bathed; they considered bathing unhealthy.

Well-to-do Chinese, on the other hand, could dress in the softest silks and sip the most fragrant tea from fragile porcelain cups. They could enjoy delicate citrus fruits such as oranges from the south. Potters produced for them exquisite objects in porcelain, and cabinetmakers made fine furniture for their houses, which were light and airy, built around open courtyards in which flowers bloomed. Marco Polo told how one of the smaller palaces of the emperor "was built of marble and other handsome stones, admirable as well for the elegance of its design as for the skill displayed in its execution." The main palace at the capital, Polo wrote, was surrounded by an outer wall that enclosed sixty-four square miles. "On each side of the four sides of the palace," he said, "there is a grand flight of marble steps, by which you ascend from the

Copper and enamel ewer from the Ming Dynasty, used for sprinkling rose water.

61

level of the ground to the wall of marble which surrounds the building, and which makes up the approach to the palace itself." Many Europeans reading Polo's book concluded that he had embroidered the tale from whole cloth, that he had told a pack of lies. Considering the comparatively low state of European civilization and Europeans' inability to imagine anything better, it is understandable that they should have felt that way.

The Chinese had invented or discovered many useful items. They had, for example, discovered gunpowder and the compass. They had invented paper-making, printing, and the seismograph for measuring earthquake strength. They had developed water-powered mills for grinding grain. In medicine the Chinese were close to discovering the idea of vaccination as a means of controlling disease long before it was developed in Europe. Chinese physicians also at an early time possessed a great deal of knowledge about anatomy. The Chinese had accurately measured the length of the year and had made other advances in astronomy. They were the first to invent such seemingly ordinary items as the stirrup and the wheelbarrow. Europeans benefitted from a number of Chinese inventions, such as the compass and the stirrup, as well as gunpowder, without knowing anything about their place of origin.

Gunpowder revolutionized warfare in Europe, but the Chinese took that and other important discoveries in stride. None of them brought drastic change to China. While the Chinese developed cannons and built seaworthy ships, they did not look upon these as means of extending their influence in the world. Europeans caught up with and surpassed the Chinese in shipbuilding, navigation, and in armament. And this development would have a vital influence on relationships between Europeans and Chinese.

Reluctantly the Chinese government allowed Europeans in to trade. After the Portuguese expulsion, ships from The Netherlands and England appeared. The Chinese government restricted them to the port of Canton, later adding the island of Macao. Although this trade was small compared to what it would become, it brought wealth to some Europeans and benefitted Chinese merchants. And, thanks to taxes, it helped the Ming government as well. Even so, that government refused to open more ports to trade, to allow it to expand.

In the eighteenth century, along with such Chinese exports as porcelain, brocades, and embroidered silks, educated Europeans began also to receive certain impressions about Chinese civilization. Much of the information came from a few Jesuit Catholic missionaries then working in China who wrote letters and reports. Europeans, particularly in France, were especially taken with Chinese philosophy and the idea that only well-educated, able men should be government officials. It became fashionable to possess Chinese art objects and to discuss and write about Confucius and Confucianism.

OPIUM TRADE AND WAR

Of all the Europeans who wished to open China to the world, the English proved the most determined. And the English, in the nineteenth century, at last achieved their goal.

The English finally made their way into China by means of opium, a black, sticky, clay-like substance obtained from the poppy plant. A narcotic, it is usually consumed in a pipe. The Dutch, or perhaps the Portuguese, first brought opium to China from India, but it was the English who used the drug to gain a firm foothold in the Middle Kingdom.

In the 1700s the English conquered India and made it a colony. They then expanded opium production, took over the trade with China, and made it highly profitable to themselves. Although the Chinese government declared the trade illegal and wished to stamp it out, corrupt government officials and merchants winked at the prohibition and reaped considerable wealth themselves.

Determined to abolish the trade, the emperor in 1839 dispatched an official named Lin Tse-hsu to Canton with orders to eliminate it. At Canton, Lin Tse-hsu seized all available opium and demanded that foreign merchants agree to deal in it no longer. The English superintendent of trade at Canton refused Lin's demand. Consequently, in December 1839 the Chinese government decreed that Englishmen could no longer trade in China. This laid a direct challenge before the British government.

In the spring of 1840 twenty British warships and troop transports appeared off Canton to blockade the port. The Opium War began.

Although the war dragged on for nearly three years, English guns and troops eventually proved too much for the Chinese. Seizing Canton, Shanghai, and other ports, the English sent gunboats up the Yangtze River nearly to Nanking. Toward the end of 1842, concluding that further fighting was useless, the Emperor Tao-kuang agreed to peace talks.

More than anything else, the British victory demonstrated that, contrary to outward appearances, China was actually a weak nation in comparison to those of Europe. China was far behind Europeans in technology. In addition, its government, controlled by the Manchus of Manchuria, who had conquered China in the 1600s and established the Ch'ing Dynasty to replace the Ming, had become corrupt and weak. The stage was set for Europeans to carve up China into "spheres of influence" and, by means of merchants backed by guns, in effect to rule that country for about a hundred years.

The Treaty of Nanking, which ended the

Opium War, forced China to pay England $21 million for the lost opium and for debts owed to British merchants. The Chinese also agreed that Britain should take over the island of Hong Kong, off the south China coast, and rule it as a colony. In addition, the treaty opened the ports of Foochow, Amoy, Ningpo, and Shanghai to British trade. The Treaty of Nanking was only the first of the unequal treaties the Chinese were forced to sign with foreign nations. Following British success, France, the United States, and other nations rushed in to claim their share of the spoils. The Chinese would pay a high price for their attitude of superiority toward foreigners.

In central China, the Yangtze valley came under British control. Russia's sphere of influence was Manchuria, later shared with the Japanese. France had southwestern China. Germany, finally, held sway in the Shantung peninsula in the northeast.

THE BURDEN OF INEQUALITY

Besides spelling out certain areas that would fall to foreign control in China, the unequal treaties forced the Chinese to agree to charge only a low tariff, or tax, on goods such as cotton thread Europeans manufactured and exported for sale in China. A low tariff helps manufacturers, frequently making it possible for them to sell goods in a foreign country at prices lower than those charged for goods produced in that country. A high tariff has the opposite effect. It tends to make domestic products cheaper, cutting out competition from foreign manufacturers.

In addition, the unequal treaties granted foreigners extraterritoriality. This meant that within their spheres of influence and within their "compounds," where they resided, Europeans would be subject to the laws of their own country, not to Chinese laws. In other words, the Chinese government enjoyed no effective control over foreigners in their midst.

The United States, acting as a friend and protector of China, enjoyed no sphere of influence itself. Americans insisted on the "open door" in China, a proposal stating that all nations should enjoy equal rights to trade there. Rather than squabble over trying to erect and enforce restrictions on each other, European nations agreed to the United States open door proposal. Although their nation had no sphere of influence, American merchants reaped great rewards from the China trade. And the American attitude toward the Chinese, which branded them as weak, inferior, and backward people, differed not at all from the opinion held by Europeans.

Along with western merchants, Christian missionaries came to China, aiming to convert the Chinese from "pagan" Taoism, Buddhism, spirit worship, their respect for ancestors, and their belief in Confucianism. Christian missionaries, both Catholic and Protestant, established schools and hospitals, and in this way brought benefits to Chinese peasants. And missionary reports to their home churches did much to make China and the Chinese known to Americans. Altogether missionaries made several million converts in China, although this, of course, represented a tiny portion of a population which by 1900 amounted to some 400 million. Owing to their religious history, most Chinese could not grasp the concept of one God. This idea was entirely foreign to their culture. Nor could they understand why, if the missionaries all believed in the same God, there should be so many different kinds of Christian faiths. There was a further objection, from the Chinese point of view. Many could not comprehend why, if a person accepted the Christian faith, he had to foresake all belief in any part of other faiths. For centuries, many Chinese had experienced no difficulty in being Taoists, Buddhists, and Confucianists all at the same

time. Each took from each religion that which suited him.

In the past, under foreign rule, Chinese had remained confident that their civilization would eventually absorb foreign invaders and that finally Chinese would rule once more. This had partially occurred during Mongol times in China and it happened under the foreign Manchus, the Ch'ing Dynasty. Both Mongols and Manchus made use of Chinese institutions, generally respecting them, ruling through government officials who were Confucian and Chinese. But now, dealing with Europeans and Americans, the Chinese faced a totally different situation. Except for missionaries, these foreigners were interested only in trade and profit. They seemed united in their attitudes toward the Chinese, and in their determination to control without much reference to the Chinese government. Except for missionaries, most foreigners were content to remain in their compounds, protected by their soldiers, and have little to do with Chinese life and culture. Under these circumstances, that Chinese civilization would absorb westerners appeared unlikely.

CONFLICTING POINTS OF VIEW

Westerners considered the Chinese hopelessly corrupt, undemocratic, and backward. Government officials and Chinese merchants frequently demanded bribes as the price of allowing business transactions to proceed smoothly. Westerners could not understand the Confucian way of life, the five relationships. They had no conception of the supremacy of the family in China, or why the Chinese viewed the group as vastly more important than the individual. Westerners dismissed reverence and respect for ancestors as foolish "worship," and they found it strange.

Westerners could not grasp the idea of an all-powerful emperor who was respected and obeyed by his subjects as was a father by his children.

Chinese and western ideas about law and individual rights differed considerably, and this lay at the heart of extraterritoriality. In China, a person accused of a crime was considered guilty until he proved himself innocent. In England and the United States, at least, the opposite assumption prevailed. According to Chinese law and custom, a poor man could be punished more severely than a member of the gentry for committing the same crime. When a prisoner came to trial, a magistrate could order that he be tortured if the magistrate did not think the man was answering questions properly. Englishmen and Americans held, at least in theory, that everyone should be treated equally under the law. In most of Europe, torture had long since gone out of style.

Westerners placed a high value on science and technology. To them, technology meant factories that produced goods for sale, ships for trade, and modern weapons to protect that trade. Westerners believed that technology would eventually bring everyone higher standards of living, in a material sense. The Chinese were much more concerned with proper relationships than with living standards. Chinese who believed firmly in the Confucian way of life could not understand the western idea of progress or westerners' desire for material wealth. Chinese could never esteem a merchant's way of life and regard it as an honorable one.

Most westerners believed in government by representatives elected by the people. In the United States especially the ability to win election was much more important than education with respect to holding public office. Although most European nations in the 1800s had kings, none of them was anywhere nearly as powerful or as respected as China's emperor. To the Chinese, it was natural that there should be an all-powerful emperor who ruled. It also seemed natural to the Chinese that inequalities among men existed, and that only well-educated men possessing ability should be government officials.

When westerners entered China, two completely opposite and stubborn civilizations clashed. One was based on the idea of inequality of proper relationships, and on obedience, respect, and obligation. It opposed the other, anchored on the idea of the importance of the individual, to some extent on political democracy, and on the concept of progress through science and technology. Few persons on either side were willing to try to understand the other. And therein lay deep and terrible tragedy.

In the 1860s China came under the rule of the mother of a five-year-old boy who became emperor when the old emperor died. Her name was Tz'u Hsi and she was, in her old age, called the Empress Dowager. She was shrewd, stubborn, ignorant, and terribly self-willed. Particularly important, the old Dowager knew how to control and manipulate government officials, keeping power firmly in her hands until her death in 1908. Although there were those in China who believed that the Chinese could rid themselves of foreign control only by reform in government and by mastering western technology, they made no impression on Tz'u Hsi. Near the end of the nineteenth century, for example, money was set aside to build a modern Chinese navy. The Empress Dowager used the funds to build a new summer palace for herself.

TAIPINGS AND COOLIE LABOR

Even before Tz'u Hsi gained power, people were reading signs that the Mandate of Heaven would soon pass from the Ch'ing Dynasty. There were floods and famines. There was starvation. Because westerners sent so much cotton thread made by machines into

China, Chinese hand spinners by the thousands were out of work. Corruption in the government grew deeper; the official examinations became objects of ridicule and laughter. Anyone who knew the right people or possessed sufficient money to pay bribes could pass them.

A number of rebellions cropped up among the peasantry, as had been the case during past times of trouble. They all came together in the Taiping Rebellion in the 1850s, the bloodiest China had ever known.

Hung Hsui-chuan, a poor scholar who had learned something about Christianity, led the Taiping Rebellion. Hung began by having visions. Then, gathering many followers, he persuaded them that they could create on earth the Heavenly Kingdom of Great Peace. They needed only to follow him, worship the Christian god, read the Bible, and obey the Ten Commandments. Hung Hsui-chuan and the Taipings did not aim simply to overthrow a dynasty. They were out to change Chinese society completely.

In areas where they gained control, the Taipings seized land from landlords and gave it to poor peasants. They wanted to build railroads and modernize China in other ways. They wished to make women equal to men and open the official examinations to women and men alike. They also formed guerrilla bands made up of women to fight government forces. Under the Taiping system, women as well as men would inherit land, and Taipings wished furthermore to abolish all cruel punishment for crimes. They would, however, punish gambling, corruption, and trading in opium very harshly.

By 1853 the Taipings had captured Wuhan, a city on the Yangtze River. Then they took Nanking, making it their capital. Before long, Taipings controlled large areas of south and central China while the Ch'ing government continued to rule in the north.

In the midst of the Taiping Rebellion En-

Chiropodist examining
a patient in the late 1800s.

gland and France battled Chinese government forces in the second Opium War. Following this, more ports were opened to foreign trade and the Chinese government agreed to allow ambassadors to live in Peking, the capital. In addition, the government agreed to supply Chinese laborers for work in European colonies around the world.

This marked the beginning of the coolie trade which saw tens of thousands of Chinese shipped to Java—an island now part of Indonesia—to work on rubber plantations, to Cuba to labor on sugar plantations, and elsewhere. *K'u-li*—muscle for hire—imported from southern China in the 1860s were mainly responsible for building that portion of the Union Pacific Railroad which ran from Sacramento, California across mountains to the Utah desert in the United States. For the most part, coolie labor was slave labor, representing another humiliation western powers visited on the Chinese.

Chinese laborers who helped build the Union Pacific Railroad in the United States were paid, but at a rate lower than that accorded white workers. Chinese immigrating to the United States faced deep white racial prejudice, especially in California, where most of them settled. Whites resented especially the Chinese willingness to work for low wages. Demands for restriction of Chinese immigration achieved success in the 1880s, when the United States Congress forbade such immigration for a period of time. This was made permanent by an act of Congress in 1924.

THE END NEARS

The second Opium War finally convinced the Ch'ing government of the superiority of western weapons. The government obtained arms from western powers and this aid, along with occasional use of foreign troops as well as corruption among the Tai-

pings themselves, eventually spelled Taiping downfall. In 1864 Nanking fell to government troops and following that, Taipings were slaughtered by the thousands. No one knows the exact figures, but somewhere between twenty and thirty million persons died during the long Taiping Rebellion. It was by far the worst civil war in the history of the world.

Taipings met defeat, and the problems they had sought to solve remained. Things simply went from bad to worse. Annam, now Vietnam, long controlled by China, was lost to the French, who made it their colony of Indochina. In 1895 China quarreled with Japan over Korea, an area which, like Annam, China had long controlled. China sent an army to Korea, Japan invaded that country, and the end swiftly came with Chinese defeat. Following the Sino-Japanese War China gave up Taiwan, the Pescadores Islands, and a portion of southern Manchuria to Japan.

Then in 1900 came the Boxer Rebellion, an uprising organized by a secret society called Righteous Harmony Fists, members of which conducted ceremonies involving dances with motions resembling shadow boxing. The Boxers aimed to rid China of foreign devils, but considering western power and the fact that the Empress Dowager connived against them, they had little chance to enjoy success. After they seized Peking, an army made up of troops from England, France, Japan, Germany, Russia, and the United States fought its way into the city and defeated them.

China, not the Boxers, paid for the rebellion. After it was put down, western nations presented the Chinese government with a bill of over $330 million to compensate them for their trouble. The government had to borrow money from foreign banks and governments to pay it, which simply tightened the western grip on China.

The end was near. The Mandate of Heaven would rest but a few more years on the Manchu dynasty known as Ch'ing.

REVOLUTION!

Westerners in gunboats opened China for trade, profit, and Christianity. But they also brought with them ideas about science, technology, and government. These ideas stirred many young Chinese who wished for a better future for their country. Eventually those men pushed China to the road of revolution, a bloody path that ancient land would travel for nearly fifty years.

Secret societies sprang up in China, each aiming to overthrow the hated Ch'ing Dynasty and modernize China. But the Ch'ing did not go down easily or with grace. The government stubbornly fought back, putting down uprisings with bloody regularity during the first decade of the twentieth century. Ten times revolutionaries tried to topple the Ch'ing. Ten times they failed. The end finally came, but almost by sheer accident. It occurred on the Day of Double Ten, the tenth day of the tenth month, October, in 1911.

In April 1911 there was an uprising in Canton. This produced little but the "Seventy-Two Martyrs," young men of the secret Yellow Flowers Hill Society killed in the fighting. In October government officials got wind of a plot in Wuhan, on the Yangtze River, obtaining also a list of names of revolutionaries involved. Then on the night of October 10, in the town of Wuchang on the Yangtze, a Chinese soldier killed his commanding officer. He and fellow soldiers then dragged a colonel out of bed and forced him to take command. Now, suddenly, there was open revolutionary activity all over China. The end, and a beginning, had arrived.

One piece was missing. The man who was to lead the revolution was not in China. Sun Yat-sen was in the United States, where he learned about the revolution from the newspapers.

A CURE FOR THE ILLS OF CHINA

Sun Yat-sen died in 1925, and sometime later his remains were buried on a hillside among the Purple and Golden Hills outside Nanking. For years afterward, people came on pilgrimages over long distances to honor the man known as the Father of the Chinese Republic. Today in China Sun Yat-sen is no longer highly thought of. The political party he began, the Kuomintang, or Nationalist Party, no longer exists there. When the Kuomintang was alive in China, its leaders were bitter enemies of the Communists who now rule the land. Sun Yat-sen helped begin a revolution, but that revolution went far beyond his plans for it.

Born the son of a peasant near Canton in

Opposite: Assistant Chief of Police at Chengtu in Szechwan province with members of the police force.   69

1866, Sun Yat-sen received his early education in the village school. At age fourteen he left China for Hawaii, living there three years with an older brother. And there Sun attended an English school and became a Christian.

Sun Yat-sen returned in 1884 to a China seething with discontent, a China which would soon lose Annam to the French and Korea to the Japanese. Sun became a revolutionary and a member of a secret society. He also studied to be a doctor and in 1892 received his degree in medicine. Sun practiced medicine only two years, after that devoting all his time to revolutionary activity and to travel in Japan, England, the United States, and elsewhere in search of support for his cause.

Aware of his activity and influence, the Ch'ing government put a price on Sun's head. And in London Ch'ing officials nearly sealed his fate. They kidnapped him and held him prisoner for several days, planning to ship him back to China for trial and almost certain execution. Sun himself knew well what was in store for him should his enemies succeed in carrying out their plans. He would meet death, he said, "first having my ankles crushed in a vise and broken by a hammer, my eyelids cut off, and finally being chopped into small fragments so that none could claim my mortal remains." The Ch'ing Dynasty was not gentle with anyone it considered traitorous, anyone who urged revolt against it.

With the aid of English friends, Sun Yat-sen escaped his captors in London. The episode made him world-famous as a leader of revolution in China.

In 1908 the Ch'ing Empress Dowager died and a three-year-old boy became emperor. The government now rested solely in the hands of palace officials. And, faced with revolution in 1911, these officials appointed a general, Yuan Shih-kai, premier and commander-in-chief of the army. But this did not save the dynasty. In February 1912 it came to an end

and by that time, Sun Yat-sen was back in China.

Thus far the revolution had been almost peaceful. There had been little fighting. This would not remain the case, however. The revolution would go on for many years. There would be savage fighting. Tens of millions of persons would die.

China was much too sick to be cured simply by a change in government. For one thing, there were the foreigners. China still was controlled by white-skinned people who all over the world looked down on black, brown, and yellow peoples as inferiors, as barbarous and backward people. Although deeply humiliated and ashamed of being treated in rough-shod ways by whites, the Chinese would find eliminating foreigners from control extremely difficult.

The Ch'ing government had been of no help in this or in other matters. That government had been hopelessly corrupt, weak, and self-serving. It should have fallen sooner than it did, but foreign nations had helped prop up the rotten carcass of a dynasty that had long since died.

Most important of all, perhaps, the Chinese peasant over the years of the Ch'ing had fallen into desperate straits. As one writer said, China was probably the only country in the world where the masses of the people were worse off than they had been five hundred years before. In China the masses of the people were peasants. They made up more than four-fifths of the total population of more than 400 million.

For centuries many peasants had suffered in the hands of tax collectors, landlords, and moneylenders. Fewer and fewer owned the land they worked. More and more lived out their lives in debt and misery. During the 1800s, things grew worse. Merchants, for example, grew rich from trade with foreign nations and many bought land with their new wealth. This forced up the price of land, making it more difficult than ever for peasants to acquire any. During past times, peasants could gain extra income by spinning cloth and by making straw hats and other items, selling them in market towns. Now many items formerly made by peasants came from foreign countries. And, thanks largely to low tariffs imposed by foreign powers, they could be purchased more cheaply in market towns than any goods produced by peasants. Peasants had to depend almost entirely on their crops for a livelihood.

And persistently there were floods and droughts to ruin the crops. Peasants, it was said, expected famine every five years. If the gods were kind, seven to ten years might pass without severe hardship. But inevitably, catastrophe struck. Then millions died, from drowning during floods, from starvation during famine that followed floods and drought.

Some peasants gave up the struggle on the land, moving to cities along the coast of China, such as Shanghai, where there were a number of factories owned by foreigners and merchants. There peasants could work fourteen hours a day for very low wages. Many others stuck it out in the countryside. Some sold daughters and wives for enough to live on for a brief time, for enough to buy seed to try to make just one more crop. Others simply joined bandit groups and lived as they could, raiding villages and towns.

No one, it seemed, cared much about peasants or, for that matter, about China either. Not westerners. Not the Ch'ing government. Not rich merchants and landlords. Only, it seemed, did some young men with vision, men who were educated and who wished their country to shed old ways and take on new. Sun Yat-sen was only one of these men. He has been the best remembered.

Sun Yat-sen wrote numerous articles explaining his ideas for a new China, ideas that were put together in a book, *Three Principles of the People,* published shortly before his death. China, Sun wrote, was weak, unedu-

cated, and divided. What would save the country and make it strong once more?

First, nationalism. The Chinese, said Sun, must develop a love and respect for their country as a nation. China must gain sufficient power to run its own affairs, which meant that foreigners would have to be driven out. Second, a people's democracy. The Chinese people would have to be educated, and eventually granted the right to vote. Then they could participate in government by electing men to represent them. Third, the people's livelihood must be assured. Peasants must own the land they worked; workers in the cities must be provided jobs by industries developed and owned by the government.

A REVOLUTION FAILS

Sun Yat-sen's ideas became the theory behind the Chinese Revolution. They outlined a means by which a new nation might be formed, a way in which China might become equal to other nations of the world.

After the fall of the Ch'ing Dynasty, Sun Yat-sen and other revolutionary leaders, having formed the Kuomintang, or Nationalist Party, set up a government. Sun was chosen president. But the new government possessed no power to unite China and make necessary changes. It lacked an army to enforce its will. And so the government finally turned to Yuan Shih-kai, a strong man with an army who had earlier served the Ch'ing government. Sun Yat-sen stepped aside and the government controlled by the Kuomintang made Yuan president. He agreed to live up to and try to carry out the ideals of the revolution. Granting power to Yuan Shih-kai marked the failure of the first stage.

Yuan Shih-kai had no intention of changing China, quickly betraying the revolution and making himself dictator. Then he decided that he would found a new dynasty and mount the

Dragon Throne as the dynasty's first emperor. Before he could carry out his plans, Yuan Shih-kai died, in 1915. Sun Yat-sen returned to the presidency.

China remained divided and Sun Yat-sen's Kuomintang remained without power. Warlords, strong men with private armies who controlled provinces, ruled the land, especially northern China. They and their soldiers lived off the produce and the taxes of the peasants. Now and then warlords fought each other, trying to expand their territories. Their principal aim was to increase their wealth and power, each hoping, perhaps, that he might eventually become supreme warlord of all China. For all purposes the feudal system, which had existed under the Chou centuries before, was now fastened on China once again. In the meantime, Europe went up in flames in World War I.

World War I began in 1914, with England, France, and Russia, and later the United States, allied against Germany and Austria-Hungary, the latter two nations at that time being joined as an empire. Fighting among themselves, European nations with interests in China could devote little attention to that area, presenting Japan with a golden opportunity. Japan moved into China to take over the Shantung peninsula, an area Germany had controlled before the war. The Japanese aimed eventually to make all China a part of an empire they planned to erect in East Asia. Next Japan laid before the Chinese government a list of what came to be known as the Twenty-one Demands, which called on China to grant Japan even more extensive rights and privileges than European nations had enjoyed. The helpless Chinese government agreed to most of the demands, which embittered many Chinese youths. The government's knuckling under to Japan's demands did much to arouse Chinese nationalism, and numerous anti-Japanese riots broke out in China.

In 1917, hoping for an Allied victory, the Chinese government declared war on Germany. China sent no troops, but it did dispatch some 200,000 coolies to labor in European war zones. By rendering sympathy and aid to the Allied cause, Chinese government leaders hoped that China might obtain a fair deal at war's end. English, French, and American leaders said they were fighting for democracy. They said that they believed that every people should have the right to choose their own government and run their own affairs. These ideas, sponsored by the American President Woodrow Wilson, inspired Chinese leaders to think that they might obtain western aid to pull China together and make it a strong nation.

Within China, writers and other intellectuals cried out for reform. Jou Shih was a writer who expressed deep dissatisfaction with the state of Chinese society and called for drastic change. He deplored in particular the sad lot of Chinese peasant women. Jou Shih's short story, "Slaves' Mother," is a good example of his work.

Her husband was a leather merchant. He bought wild-animal skins from the village hunters and oxhides to sell in the big city. Sometimes he did a little farming too, helping transplant rice-seedlings in the spring. He could plant so straight a row that if five others were working in a paddy-field with him they put him at the end of the line as marker. But things were always against him; his debts piled up over the years. It was probably because everything had gone so badly that he had taken to opium, drink, and gambling, which had finally turned him into a cruel and loutish fellow, poorer than ever and no longer able even to raise a small loan to tide them over.

His destitution brought with it a disease that turned him a withered yellow-brown all over: his face went the color of a little bronze drum, and even the whites of his eyes turned brown. People said that he had the yellow liver sickness, and the children called him Yellow Fatty.

One day he said to his wife, "There's nothing for it. If we go on this way we'll even be selling our little cooking pots before long. Looks as though you'll have to provide the solution. No use your staying and starving with me."

"Me?" his wife asked dully. She was sit-

The poor of Nanking collect lotus roots for fuel.

ting behind the stove holding her baby boy, now just three years old, as she fed him at her breast.

"Yes, you." Her husband's voice was weak with sickness. "I've pledged you."

"What?" His wife almost fainted. There was a moment of silence in the room before he continued, gasping for breath, "Wolf Wang came here three days ago and went on and on demanding that money back. When he went I followed him as far as the Two Acre Pond. I wanted to do myself in. I sat under the tree you can jump into the pond from and thought and thought, but I didn't have the strength to jump. Besides, an owl was hooting in my ear, and it made me so scared I came home. On the way back I met Mrs. Shen who asked me why I was out so late. I told her everything and asked her to borrow some money for me or some clothes or jewelry from a girl that I could pawn to keep Wolf Wang's wolf-eyes from glaring around the house every day.

"She said, 'Why are you keeping your wife at home? Look how sick you are yourself.' I couldn't say anything, just looked at the ground, but she went on, 'You've only got one son, and you couldn't spare him. But what about your wife?' I thought she was going to tell me to sell you—'Even though you are married there's no other option when you're hard up. Why keep her at home?'

"Then she said straight out, 'There's a gentleman of fifty who has no son and wants to marry a second wife. His first wife won't agree, and will only let him hire one for three or four years. He's asked me to look out for a suitable woman. She must be about thirty and have had two or three children. She must be quiet, well-behaved, hard-working, and willing to obey the first wife. The gentleman's wife told me that if these conditions were met they'd pay eighty or a hundred dollars for her. I've been looking for someone for several days but I can't find the right woman.'

"Then she said that meeting me made her think of you: you're just what's wanted. She asked me what I thought about it and forced me to agree though the tears were in my eyes."

"Is it settled?" the woman asked, her teeth chattering.

"As soon as the contract's signed."

"Curse it. Is . . . is there no other way out, Chunbao's dad?"

Chunbao was the name of the child she was hugging.

"I've thought it over and over. But we're so poor we'll have to do it to stay alive. I don't even know whether I'll be able to transplant rice this year."

"Have you thought about Chunbao? He's only three—he can't do without his mum."

"I'll keep him—you've weaned him."

He had gradually lost his temper. When he walked out through the door she began to sob.

In tears, Yellow Fatty's wife reflected on the birth of her last child, a girl. She had given birth without assistance but, lying on her bed as the baby rested on a pile of straw, she was too weak to arouse herself to wash it. Her husband appeared with a bucket of boiling water. Without a word he took the infant and plunged it into the water, murdering it.

Leaving her three-year-old boy, the wife went to live in the well-to-do scholar's house. There she suffered from loneliness, worry about Chunbao, and from jealousy and hatred of the scholar's first wife. In due time she presented the scholar with a child, a boy. She fulfilled the contract and was at last, after three years, allowed to return home.

At what seemed to be about three or four in the afternoon an uncovered sedan chair was carried down a narrow, dirty village street. In the chair lay a middle-aged woman with a face as shrivelled as a dried-up cabbage leaf. Her eyes were half shut with exhaustion and her breathing was weak. The people in the street all gazed at her with astonishment and pity, and a crowd of children followed the chair shouting and yelling. It was as if something strange had arrived in the silent village.

Chunbao was one of the children following the chair. He was shouting as if he were driving a pig, but when the chair turned into the lane leading to his own home he stretched out his hands in amazement. Then it reached his front gate. He stood stock still, leaning on a pillar some way away from it. The other children stood timidly on either side of the chair. As the woman stepped out her eyes were too blurred to recognize her own Chunbao, the six-year-old boy in ragged clothes and with matted hair who was no taller than he had been three years ago. Then suddenly she started crying and called "Chunbao."

The children were startled. Chunbao was so frightened that he went indoors to hide in his father's room.

The woman sat in the murky room for a very long time. Neither she nor her husband spoke. As night fell his drooping head straightened up and he said: "Cook us a meal."

She had to get up. After walking round the room she said weakly to her husband:

"The rice jar is empty."

Her husband laughed bitterly. "You really have been living with the gentry. The rice is in that cigarette tin."

That evening her husband said to her son: "Go sleep with your mother, Chunbao."

But Chunbao started to cry in the alcove. His mother went up to him, calling him by

his name, but when she tried to caress him he dodged away from her.

"I'll hit you for forgetting her as fast as that," said her husband to him. She lay with her eyes wide open on a dirty and narrow plank bed with Chunbao lying beside her like a stranger. In her numbed brain a fat and lovable Qiubao [the child by the scholar] was fidgeting beside her, but when she put out her hands to hug him he turned out to be Chunbao. Chunbao, now asleep, turned over. His mother hugged him tight, and as he snored lightly he lay his head on her chest, stroking her breasts with his hands.

The long night, as cold and lonely as death, dragged interminably on and on.

Despite hope for change among writers such as Jou Shih, participation in World War I helped China not at all. The Allied nations won, but their victory brought no aid to the Chinese. Nothing changed, except that Japan instead of Germany now possessed influence in China. Chinese students took to the streets in anti-foreign riots and demonstrations. Chinese leaders looked elsewhere for assistance. They turned to the Soviet Union.

TWO LEADERS RISE

Russia in 1917 had had its own revolution, with Communists winning control of that vast land. Russian Communists were willing to help foment revolutions everywhere, and they sent advisors and some arms and other aid to Sun Yat-sen's government in China.

With Russian advice and aid, the Sun Yat-sen government established a military academy along the muddy bank of the Whampoa River near Canton, intending to develop the armed power needed to bring about the change the government wished in China. To direct the

Whampoa Military Academy, Sun Yat-sen chose a favorite young army officer, Chiang Kai-shek.

Chiang Kai-shek was born in 1887 in the province of Chekiang, in south China. For many generations, the Chiang family had been peasants. Chiang's grandfather, however, became a salt merchant and his son, Chiang's father, followed him in the business. The family was not wealthy, but it lived comfortably until, when Chiang was nine, his father died and his mother had to bring him up alone on much less income.

After receiving a Confucian education, Chiang attended a military school. Then he spent three years in Japan learning more military science. Upon returning to China, Chiang joined the revolutionary movement and he later married Soong Mei-ling, daughter of a wealthy merchant-banker. Sun Yat-sen himself married another Soong daughter, the elder sister of Mei-ling. And, like Sun, Chiang Kai-shek became a Christian. This slender, proud, and somber man would play an important role in the history of modern China. So would another, a round-faced man with an ambling gait, also a native of south China.

In the summer of 1921, a group of revolutionaries met in Shanghai to form the Chinese Communist Party. Harassed by the police, the men moved their meeting place to a boat on a lake at Chiashing, near Shanghai, where they completed the party's organization. Among those on board the boat that July day was a young man named Mao Tse-tung, until then an assistant librarian in Peking.

Born the son of a peasant in 1893 in Hunan province, like Chiang Kai-shek Mao Tse-tung received a Confucian education. However, he preferred reading historical novels to memorizing Confucian classics. At age thirteen Mao had to leave school to help his father full time on the family farm. Later, he attended a higher school in Changsha. When the revolution broke out in 1911, Mao joined it and for a brief time served in a revolutionary army, later participating in the student demonstrations that followed World War I. He spent some time in jail for that. As western nations turned their backs on China, Mao, like many other young revolutionaries, gravitated to Communism as a solution to China's problems. They read, studied, and discussed Communist ideas and the Communist success in Russia. By the summer of 1920 Mao Tse-tung had become, in theory and to some extent in action, a Communist. Certainly from that time on he considered himself a Communist.

Chinese Communists and Sun Yat-sen's group, the Kuomintang, shared certain goals. Both wanted a strong and united China. Both wanted China freed from foreign control. To achieve these goals, according to the Communist point of view, thoroughgoing revolution would be necessary, bringing about drastic change in Chinese society. Private ownership of property would have to be abolished. The people, through their government, would own not only all the land but factories and transportation and communication systems as well. There no longer would be landlords, rich or poor, or factory owners, merchants, and moneylenders who operated for personal profit. The people, led by the Communist Party, would rule China. Such a revolution had occurred in Russia following Communist triumph there and the establishment of a Communist dictatorship. This was the kind of change Chinese Communists intended to promote in their country.

At first, though, Communists did not push their ideas hard. Although by 1927 the Chinese Communist Party held about 58,000 members, during the early 1920s it had only a few hundred.

Some members of the Kuomintang tended to agree with the Communists' ideas, at least in part, while others did not. Certain members advocated change, but not drastic change, preferring to rely on support from landlords and merchants, not on peasants and workers in the cities.

Yet numerous observers believed that what China needed at the time, first of all and more than anything else, was land reform and relief for peasants. And it appeared that this could occur only through strong government action to force gentry and other landlords to give up some of their holdings and distribute land, through sale or outright grant, to landless peasants. No one seemed to believe it likely that landlords would willingly surrender land, accepting change.

Chiang Kai-shek, however, had two objectives in mind which he considered of paramount and pressing importance. First of all, he wished to eliminate warlord control in China, which hampered the country's progress, and unify the nation under the Kuomintang and his leadership. Once that had been accomplished, Chiang would turn his attention to his second goal: removing China from foreign domination which had persisted since the middle of the nineteenth century. Only by realizing these two objectives, Chiang Kai-shek believed, could the goals of the Chinese revolution be achieved. Concentrating on warlords first, and foreigners second, Chiang did not give immediate attention to problems with which peasants were concerned, such as land reform.

For a time the Kuomintang and the Communists worked together to promote the Chinese Revolution. Communists were allowed to join the Kuomintang as individual members and, in the meantime, the Party was free to increase its membership.

Following Sun Yat-sen's death in 1925, Chiang Kai-shek took over as Kuomintang leader. Chiang now gathered his army to march against the warlords, aiming to reclaim China from them and make it a united country under his leadership. In the spring of 1926, Chiang began his Northern Expedition. Sweeping northward from Canton to the Yangtze valley, Chiang's Nationalist troops moved eastward down the valley, taking Hankow, next Nanking. Then they marched on Shanghai.

According to Communist theory—and the Russian example—revolution in a country would begin with and depend on urban workers who could be organized, disciplined, and directed, and who were vitally important to any nation that would industrialize. Revolution in Russia had begun and succeeded in the cities without much reference to the peasantry. Chinese Communist Party leaders in the 1920s followed the Russian Communist lead, and Russian advisors insisted that they concentrate on organizing the workers. The Russians knew nothing and cared even less about Chinese peasants. Consequently Communists in Shanghai in particular organized factory and other workers, and in the spring of 1927, as Chiang and his army approached, Communists seized the city. They then turned it over to Chiang.

Chiang Kai-shek surprised the Communists in Shanghai. He had concluded that they and the Kuomintang could no longer work together, for he was convinced that the Communists planned to seize control of all China. Consequently he ordered his soldiers to attack Communists in Shanghai, and some three hundred of them were killed. Later in 1927, Communists in Canton attempted to take over that city. Once again Kuomintang soldiers fought them, this time killing about five thousand. The brief period of Communist-Kuomintang cooperation came to an end.

Not only Chiang Kai-shek, but landlords, gentry, and merchants also feared and hated Communists. They knew that if Communists grew sufficiently powerful they would take land and other property from owners. Lines of conflict between Communists and the Kuomintang now were sharply drawn. There was no way the Kuomintang and the Communists could get together. The Kuomintang government outlawed the Communist Party.

END OF THE KUOMINTANG

The Shanghai and Canton experiences convinced Mao Tse-tung that the cities would never serve as a firm base for Communist revolution in China, and here he parted company with Russian advisors. They remained unable to perceive, as Mao did, the value and the urgency of organizing the Chinese peasantry. Mao had moved to this conclusion following a visit to several provinces in 1926, some six months before the Shanghai disaster.

According to historians of the period, Mao became convinced that in China's central, southern, and northern provinces the peasants, if encouraged, would rise up in revolution. They would, he believed, sweep away all imperialists, warlords, corrupt officials, local strongmen, and members of the gentry who oppressed them. So, it seemed to Mao, three choices lay at hand. A person could place himself at the peasantry's head, leading and directing peasants toward certain goals. Or he might trail behind, allowing them to take the lead. Or he might oppose them, trying to turn back the tide.

Sun Yat-sen, the original maker of revolution in China, had based his movement mainly on the intellectuals and the middle class. He drew most of his support for revolution from near the top. Mao, however, was of peasant background. He believed that he understood peasant problems, desires, and ways of thinking. He wished further revolution in China, and he did not think it would succeed without peasant support and involvement. Consequently he decided to begin his revolution at the bottom, basing it on the peasantry.

Not a highly industrialized country, China, lacked a large urban working class. And Chiang Kai-shek, determined to eliminate Communists as a factor in Chinese life, was able to defeat them in the cities. Communists then retreated to the countryside. Mao Tse-tung and others, including Generals Ch'en Yi, Lin Piao, and Chu Teh, organized groups in the mountains of Hunan and Kiangsi provinces in south central China. Needing support, as part of their overall strategy Communists tended to treat poor peasants well. Landlords who resisted Communist domination, however, received harsh treatment. Their land was taken from them and turned over to poor peasants, as was that of some middle peasants.

According to historians, Communist strategy with respect to poor peasants worked. In addition to giving land to tenant farmers and landless laborers, the Communists insisted their their armies maintain good rela-

Opposite: Chinese commandos taking part in a military exercise in Fukien province a few years before the Communist revolution.

tions with the poor peasants.

Communists formed Peasant Associations in the Kiangsi Soviet. And during the course of bringing peasants around to the Communist point of view, a number of brutal excesses were committed. Landlords were harassed and some—no one knows how many—were killed. Numerous middle peasants were treated unfairly as land was taken from them. Some farm equipment and crops were destroyed.

As Communist control tightened, however, and as leaders exerted more discipline on followers, terror and excess appear to have diminished. Leaders hoped that lighter treatment would bring more middle peasants into the Associations. Some observers later came to believe that in siding with poor peasants and carrying out land reform, Mao and other Communist leaders found the key to their support and cooperation. And these observers also concluded that, with peasant aid, Communists in Kiangsi developed the nucleus of a Chinese Communist society.

ATTEMPTS TO SUBDUE COMMUNISTS

Communists in Kiangsi posed a serious problem for Chiang Kai-shek. During the next several years, as the 1920s closed and the 1930s opened, he devoted much attention to them. In the meantime, in 1929 especially, millions of Chinese suffered famine. One American newspaperman, describing famine scenes, could not understand why the Chinese did not revolt against harsh landlords, warlords, and Kuomintang generals some people considered corrupt:

In those hours of nightmare I spent in Sui-yuan, I saw thousands of men, women and children starving to death before my eyes. I don't mean to dramatize horror. Millions of people died that way in famine. But these were not the most shocking things after all. The most shocking thing was that in many of those towns there were still rich men, rice hoarders, wheat hoarders, moneylenders, and landlords, with armed guards to defend them, while they profiteered enormously. The shocking thing was that in the cities—where officials danced or played with sing-song girls—there was grain and food, and had been for months; that in Peking and Tientsin and elsewhere were thousands of tons of wheat and millet collected (most by contributions from abroad) by the Famine Commission, but which could not be shipped to the starving. Why not? Because in the northwest there were some militarists who wanted to hold all their rolling stock [railroad cars] and would release none of it toward the east, while in the east there were Kuomintang generals who would send no rolling stock westward—even to starving people—because they feared it would be seized by their rivals.

Yet the great majority of those people who died did so without an act of protest! "Why don't they revolt?" I asked myself. "Why don't they march in a great army and attack the scoundrels who can tax them but cannot feed them, or who can seize their lands but cannot repair an irrigation canal? Or why don't they sweep into the great cities, and plunder the wealth of the rascals who buy their daughters and wives, the men who continue to gorge themselves on elaborate thirty-six-course banquets while honest men starve? Why not?"

I was profoundly puzzled by their lack of action. For a while I thought nothing would make a Chinese fight.

I was mistaken. The Chinese peasant is not passive; he is not a coward. He will fight when he is given a method, an organization, leadership, a workable program, hope—and arms.

Chiang Kai-shek conducted five of what he called "bandit extermination" campaigns against Communists in Hunan and Kiangsi provinces. And Communists fought back fiercely. Chiang's superior forces tended to win pitched battles, when two armies faced each other squarely. But Communists tried to avoid such confrontations whenever possible. They utilized guerrilla warfare instead. When Chiang's men advanced, Communists tended to retreat and avoid contact with them. But when his forces withdrew from a spot, Communists attacked. And when Kuomintang armies halted and went into camp, Communists, moving quickly and silently, struck with hit-and-run raids. Despite the armed might Chiang Kai-shek poured into Communist-held areas, he was unable to subdue or dislodge his enemies. The fact that Communists used guerrilla tactics in difficult terrain had much to do with this; they were difficult to pin down.

But in the Hunan and Kiangsi mountains, the Communists could not hold out forever. Time was running out for them. And so on October 16, 1934, 100,000 of them broke out from the encircling Kuomintang armies. They headed west, then south, then north on the Long March of six thousand miles to Shensi province, in northcentral China.

It is difficult to look upon the epic Long March as anything but a feat of incredible courage, determination, hardship, and success. The Red Army and thousands of men, thirty-five women, and a few children crossed raging streams, dug through snow-packed mountain passes, limped over burning deserts, and sloshed and slid through swamps that stretched for miles. All the while the Red Army fought off attacks from Kuomintang troops and from savage tribesmen who hated all Chinese. A skirmish large or small occurred almost every day. There were more than a dozen pitched battles. Entrusting three of his children to peasants along the way, Mao Tse-tung never heard from them again.

Only some three thousand Communists un-der Mao Tse-tung reached Shensi province in October 1935 after 368 days on the march. There they recuperated, built their strength, and planned the future.

WAR WITH THE JAPANESE

As Chinese fought Chinese, the Japanese, who had gained a firm foothold during World War I, inched ever more deeply into China. The Japanese government had been taken over by militarists who gradually established dictatorial rule and began to develop plans for what they called the Greater East Asia Co-Prosperity Sphere, an empire into which Japanese military leaders planned to incorporate China as well as other countries in East Asia. The Japanese stationed an army, the Kwantung, in Manchuria to guard Japanese interests there.

In September 1931 Kwantung Army leaders engineered an incident. Having a portion of a railroad line blown up by secret agents, they then blamed Chinese troops in the area for the deed. This signalled a general attack and by early 1932 Japanese troops controlled all Manchuria. With its thirty million people that area, formerly Chinese, became a Japanese colony. Japan renamed Manchuria Manchukuo. Japanese leaders now laid plans for further Chinese conquest. The Japanese began to bite off more and more Chinese territory south of the Great Wall. They encouraged the Chinese to war on each other, realizing that this would keep China weak and make the Japanese task of conquest easier.

To the Communists, it was tragically absurd that Chinese should fight Chinese while the Japanese threatened to take over all of China. Communists called on Chinese to unite against the hated Japanese. Many of Chiang Kai-shek's generals agreed, convinced too that China rested in grave danger from Japan. The campaign against the Communists gradually ground to a halt.

This was not, however, to Chiang Kai-shek's liking. He too hated the Japanese and he too wished a united China. But first he intended to smash his immediate enemies, the Communists. Then he would build up China's industries and his army and finally face the Japanese. Chiang in 1936 flew to Sian, in Shensi province, to try to persuade warlord generals to continue the Kuomintang struggle against Mao's Communist forces. And there Chiang was kidnapped, not by Communists, but by warlords who wanted to fight the Japanese.

Held prisoner for two weeks, Chiang Kai-shek met with Chou En-lai, Mao's chief lieutenant, and other Communist leaders. Out of these meetings came an agreement for joint Communist-Kuomintang action against the Japanese. The civil war would halt. Chiang further agreed that changes would be made in China according to ideas outlined by Sun Yat-sen in his *Three Principles of the People*.

COOPERATION DASHED

The Sian agreement hardly pleased the Japanese, for they now faced a united China and would have to alter their timetable of conquest and step up their efforts. And so in July 1937, near the Marco Polo Bridge in Peking, Japanese and Chinese soldiers clashed. The fighting quickly spread. Full scale war between Japan and China now began.

Chinese soldiers fought bravely and well when they possessed guns, supplies, and proper leadership. But good subordinate leadership was often lacking, and frequently soldiers lacked equipment that would allow them to stand up to Japan's modern guns and warplanes. The Japanese took Shanghai, Nanking, Peking, and other cities on or near the coast of China. They moved inland along the Yangtze River. Chiang Kai-shek retreated further and further into the interior, finally making his capital at Chungking, deep in southwestern China. In the north, Communists carried on guerrilla warfare against the Japanese. It was at this time that Norman Bethune, a Canadian doctor, joined Mao's group, organizing mobile hospital units to care for the wounded.

Chiang Kai-shek realized that Communists would continue to present a severe problem to him. He knew that one day he would renew battle with them. As he said in 1941: "I tell you that it is more important that I have kept Communists from spreading. The Japanese are a disease of the skin; the Communists are a disease of the heart. They say they want to support me, but secretly they want to overthrow me."

THE CONFLICT WIDENS

The Japanese held the coast of China. They held areas along some rivers. They bombed Chungking regularly, but they could not break the spirit of the people there. The Japanese made little progress in the interior of China. They could not conquer the vast land.

In areas they occupied, the Japanese behaved with unbelievable cruelty. After capturing Nanking in 1937, uncontrolled by officers, Japanese soldiers ran amok, raping, killing, and destroying. In the countryside they seized food, animals, and supplies from peasants, treating them harshly when they could not comply with demands for more. In occupied China the Japanese did nothing to endear themselves to the people. The gentry in many areas, testing the wind, withdrew from sight as the Japanese took over. When it appeared to them that the Japanese were there to stay, many gentry collaborated with them. This added yet another poisoned arrow to the store of peasants' bitterness toward the gentry—a bitterness which would eventually be turned full force against them.

Two years after the Japanese invasion of China, in 1939, the flames of war began to rage once more in Europe. As Japan had become a military dictatorship, so had dictators taken control in Italy and Germany, Benito Mussolini in 1922 in the former, Adolf Hitler in 1933 in the latter. Hitler aimed to gain revenge for Germany's defeat in World War I, and he built up Germany's army, navy, and air force, seeking to conquer all of Europe. In the spring of 1938 Germany took over neighboring Austria. That fall, Hitler demanded, and obtained, a portion of Czechoslovakia, a new country in central Europe formed after World War I. Although opposed to Hitler, neither England nor France did anything about his moves in Europe, nor did they act against Germany in the spring of 1939 when Germany took over the remainder of Czechoslovakia. In the fall, however, when on September 1, 1939 Germany invaded Poland, France and England did act, declaring war on Germany. World War II, which really had begun with Japan's seizure of Manchuria in 1931, certainly with that country's invasion of China six years later, now engulfed Europe as well.

England, France, and The Netherlands held colonies in Asia—the Malay peninsula, India, Burma, Indochina, and what were known as the Dutch East Indies, now Indonesia. Japan, wishing to obtain control of such raw materials as rubber and oil which these colonies held, sought to take them over. Only one obstacle stood in the way: the United States.

Although not wishing to engage in war itself, the United States sympathized with China, condemning Japanese aggression there and aiding Chiang Kai-shek with arms, money, and supplies. The United States also aided England, struggling alone in Europe against Germany. The American people did not want their country in the war. But most did want their government to do all it could short of war to help England and China.

However, as the Japanese eyed French, British, and Dutch colonies in Asia, the United States assumed a firm stand against Japanese ambitions in that direction. At the same time the United States demanded that Japan remove itself from China. Japanese leaders concluded that they could not achieve their goals in Asia until the United States, which kept a powerful fleet in the Pacific based in Hawaii, was eliminated as a threat. The result was a surprise Japanese air attack on Pearl Harbor, a naval base in Hawaii, on December 7, 1941. The daring raid was highly successful, Japanese planes sinking or severely damaging several major United States battleships and killing several thousand people. Pearl Harbor brought the United States into World War II and a few days after that December 7, Italy and Germany declared war on the United States, giving that nation a two-front conflict.

China's war now became America's war. Chiang Kai-shek confidently assumed an American victory over Japan and rested assured that his days of fighting Japanese were definitely over. And he was right. Organizing its industrial might, its factories pouring out warplanes, ships, arms, and other war materiel, its army expanding rapidly, the United States gradually turned the tide of war in the Pacific. United States forces took one after another Japanese-held island, inching ever closer to the home islands themselves. In the meantime American forces devastated Japanese cities with aerial bombardment. Then on August 6, 1945, a United States warplane loosed an atomic bomb over the Japanese city of Hiroshima, destroying it and killing 78,000 people. Three days later, the United States dropped another nuclear bomb on Nagasaki. Faced with such destructive weapons, on August 14, 1945 Japan surrendered. The Pacific War was over, the war in Europe having ended with United States, English, French, and Russian victory the previous May.

THE FALL OF CHIANG

China had suffered through eight long years of war. It would experience further bitter conflict, for the final bloody stage of Communist-Kuomintang struggle now began, to endure for nearly four more years.

The end of World War II found China in a state of near total collapse. Communists controlled much of the north, while some areas the Kuomintang held suffered from confusion and disorganization. Added to this, millions of Chinese suffered and died from famine which swept through several provinces in 1945. American reporter Theodore White described how in Honan province "People chipped at bark, pounded it by the roadside for food; vendors sold leaves at a dollar a bundle. A dog digging at a mound was exposing a human body. Ghostlike men were skimming the stagnant pools to eat the green slime of the waters." The Kuomintang government was unable to get food to the famine areas to relieve the suffering.

Throughout the war, warlords had ruled parts of China. They extracted much from peasants in the way of food and taxes. To warlords, the war at most had been an inconvenience. They suffered little. Peasants suffered though. And according to reports from observers on the scene, they could not understand why the Kuomintang government did not do something about their plight, why it did not control the warlords.

In contrast to warlords, Communists sought to win peasants to their side by treating them well. Under instructions from leaders, whenever using peasant houses Red Army soldiers were to return straw matting used as mattresses. They were also to give back any other articles they had borrowed from peasants, and pay good prices for things they purchased. Further, they were to replace all damaged goods. Above all, they were to be honest in all dealings with peasants, and treat them courteously and politely.

Both Chiang and Mao had fought the Japanese. And each believed that he should be China's leader at war's end. All nations recognized Chiang and the Kuomintang as China's rightful government. But Mao believed that the Communists had borne the brunt of fighting the Japanese. Said he in 1945:

To whom should the fruits of victory belong? It is very obvious. Take a peach tree, for example. When the tree yields peaches, they are the fruits of victory. Who is entitled to pick the peaches? Ask, who planted and watered the tree? Chiang Kai-shek, squatting on the mountain, did not carry a single bucket of water and yet he is now stretching out his arms from afar to pick the peaches. I, Chiang Kai-shek, own these peaches, he says. I am the landlord, you are my peasants, and I won't allow you to pick any. We say, you never carried any water, so you have no right to pick the peaches. We, the people of the liberated areas, watered the tree day in and day out, and have the most right to gather the fruit. Comrades, the victory of the war of resistance against the Japanese has been won by the people with bloodshed and sacrifice. It should be the victory of the people and it is to the people that the fruits of the war of resistance should go. As for Chiang Kai-shek, he was passive in resisting Japan but active in anticommunism. He was a stumbling block. Now this stumbling block is coming forward to take over the fruits of victory. We will not tolerate this. This gives rise to struggle. Comrades, it is a most serious struggle.

Considering Chiang Kai-shek China's lawful ruler, the United States government did not agree with Mao. The American government had fully supported the Kuomintang, and it had extended a great deal of aid to Chiang in the form of money, arms, and supplies during World War II. It continued to support Chiang after the war as the Kuomintang-Communist struggle to control all of China began in earnest.

Shortly before World War II ended, as an ally of the United States the Soviet Union had declared war on Japan, moving troops into Manchuria. Later it was alleged in the United States that by taking over Manchuria, the Russians, as they had planned to do all along, helped Mao Tse-tung toward eventual victory. Actually the Russians gave Mao precious little help, if any at all. They doubted his strength and they doubted seriously the possibility of Communist success in China because of the peasant base Mao had given the revolution. The Russians nurtured equally grave reservations about the strength of Chiang, but the Soviet Union continued to support him officially. Russians disarmed Japanese troops in Manchuria and some of these arms eventually fell into Communist hands. Russians turned Manchurian territory over to Kuomintang troops, however, not to Communist forces. And the Russians dismantled many factories in Manchuria, carting a great deal of industrial equipment off to Russia, a move scarcely designed to help either Mao or Chiang, but of great advantage to the Soviet Union. Mao's forces had to fight Kuomintang troops to win Manchuria, and they did so successfully.

The United States government attempted to work out a compromise between Chiang and the Communists, but this proved impossible. Consequently, in 1947, concluding that regardless of the amount of help he received Chiang could not win the civil war, the United States cut off aid to him.

By the end of 1948 Communist troops had won Manchuria. They then moved south. According to reports, thousands of Kuomintang soldiers laid down their arms, some joining the Communist side. In the summer of 1949 the Communists were in Peking. There they were ordered to march out of their way to parade through the foreign legation, the portion of the city formerly controlled by foreigners. This apparently was a symbolic gesture to show that foreign supremacy in China was at an end. Chiang Kai-shek and a part of his army retreated to Taiwan, also known as Formosa, an island off the south coast of China. There Chiang continued his Kuomintang government. What came to be known as Mainland China now was Communist. Some nations, including Canada and Britain, recognized the Communist government as legitimate. The United States, however, did not.

A NEW SOCIETY

"**A** revolution," it has been said, "is not the same as inviting people to dinner, or writing an essay, or painting a picture, or doing fancy needlework; it cannot be anything so restrained and magnanimous. A revolution is an uprising, an act of violence whereby one class overthrows another."

By the summer of 1949, after many years of struggle, Communists had won control, establishing the People's Republic of China. Far-reaching change resulted.

The gentry and rich peasants bore the brunt of change in the countryside. One example from the village of Changchuang—Long Bow—typifies what all China experienced during the first years of Communist rule.

Landlord Sheng Ching-ho, the richest man in oden door that was the sole entrance to Ch'ung-to the angry shouts of the people as they accud to open it he was seized from behind by several After dark Ching-ho crept out onto the street athe village, sat at home all that day and listened something about what had happened. Perhapssed Ch'ung-wang and swarmed over his house. new offensive. He knocked quietly on the wond stole to Ch'ung-wang's door, hoping to learn wang's courtyard, but before anyone appeare some plan could be worked out to counter this militiamen [Communist soldiers] and dragged off to the village lockup. It was then two days before the Chinese New Year. The wealthy families had planned all sorts of good things to eat and their wives and servants had been preparing and cooking for days. The leaders of the Peasants' Association decided not to let Ching-ho pass such a happy holiday. They set the attack on him for the next day, even though that meant they had no time to mobilize opinions against him. As it happened, a blunder on the part of Ching-ho's brother, Sheng Ching-chung, aroused the people more than several days of mobilization could possibly have done.

As soon as Sheng Ching-chung heard that his brother Ching-ho had been detained, he took a bag of wheat flour on his shoulder and went calling. He found the [new] assistant village head, Kuei-ts'ai, at home talking with San-ch'ing, the village secretary. He set his bag of flour by the door, greeted them both warmly, and sat himself down to have a friendly chat. It did not take him long to get to the point. "I know your life is hard," he said. "Since we are people of one village, please do not stand on ceremony but help yourselves to this flour and pass a happy New

Year. Later on, if you should meet with any difficulties, you should know that my door is always open and I am always ready to help."

The two young cadres [*kanpu,* meaning "backbone personnel" or leader, referring to both individuals and groups] could hardly believe their eyes and ears. What did he take them for—rats who could be bought with a bag of flour? They drove him and his burden out of the house and went immediately to T'ien-ming. The next afternoon Kuei-ts'ai and San-ch'ing told a village-wide meeting how Ching-chung had tried to bribe them. Their story aroused a storm of protest and a flood of accusations.

"In the famine year he gave us nothing. He even drove beggars away from his door, but now suddenly he weeps for our hard life—now we are 'people of one village,'" said one.

"It is clear he only wants to buy off the leaders and undermine our ranks. We should never be taken in by such tricks," added another.

"This should be a lesson to all of us," said T'ien-ming. "Never trust a landlord; never protect a landlord. There is only one road and that is to struggle against them."

The cadres had been afraid that the people might hold back their accusations against Ching-ho, but Kuei-Ts'ai's report broke the dam. There was no holding back. Over 100 grievances were registered at that one meeting. So vicious had been Ching-ho's practices and so widespread his influence that more than half of the families in the village had scores to settle with him.

What happened on the following day was told to me by Kuo Cheng-k'uan, Chairman of the Peasants' Association:

When the final struggle began Ching-ho was faced not only with those hundred accusations but with many, many more. Old women who had never spoken in public before stood up to accuse him. Even Li Mao's wife—a woman so pitiable she hardly dared look anyone in the face—shook her fist before his nose and cried out, "Once I went to glean wheat on your land. But you cursed me and drove me away. Why did you curse and beat me? Why did you seize the wheat I had gleaned?" Altogether over 180 opinions were raised. Ching-ho had no answer to any of them. He stood there with his head bowed. We asked him whether the accusations were false or true. He said they were all true. When the committee of our Association met to figure up what he owed, it came to 400 bags of milled grain, not coarse millet.

That evening all the people went to Ching-ho's courtyard to help take over his property. It was very cold that night, so we built bonfires and the flames shot up toward the stars. It was very beautiful. We went in to register his grain and altogether found but 200 bags of unmilled millet—only half of what he owed us. Right then and there we decided to call another meeting. People all said he must have a lot of silver dollars—they thought of the wine plant, and the pigs he raised on the distillers' grains, and the North Temple Society and the Confucius Association.

We called him out of the house and asked him what he intended to do since the grain was not nearly enough. He said, "I have land and a house."

"But all this is not enough," shouted the people. So then we began to beat him. Finally he said, "I have 40 silver dollars under the *k'ang*" [a brick surface warmed from below by a stove]. We went in and dug it up. The money stirred up everyone. We beat him again. He told us where to find another hundred dollars after that. But no one believed that this was the end of his hoard. We beat him again and several militiamen began to heat an iron bar in one of the fires. Then Ching-ho admitted that he had hidden 110 silver dollars in militiaman Man-hsi's uncle's home. Man-hsi was very hot-headed. When he heard that his uncle had helped Sheng Ching-ho he got very angry. He ran home and began to beat his father's own brother. We stopped him. We told him, "Your uncle didn't know it was a crime." We asked the old man why he had hidden money for Ching-ho and he said, "No one ever told me anything. I didn't know there was anything wrong in it." You see, they were relatives and the money had been given to him for safekeeping years before. So Man-hsi finally cooled down. It was a good thing, for he was angry enough to beat his uncle to death and he was strong enough to do it.

Altogether we got $500 from Ching-ho that night. By that time the sun was already rising in the eastern sky. We were all tired and hungry, especially the militiamen who had called the people to the meeting, kept guard on Ching-ho's house, and taken an active part in beating Ching-ho and digging for the money. So we decided to eat all the things that Ching-ho had prepared to pass the New Year—a whole crock of dumplings stuffed with pork and peppers and other delicacies. He even had shrimp.

All said, "In the past we never lived through a happy New Year because he always asked for his rent and interest then and cleaned our houses bare. This time we'll eat what we like," and everyone ate his fill and didn't even notice the cold.

That was one of the happiest days the people of Long Bow ever experienced. They were in such a mellow mood that they released Ching-ho on the guarantee of a relative, let him remain at home unguarded, and called off the struggle for the rest of the holiday season.

But Ching-ho did not wait around to see what would happen when action resumed. He ran away the very next day. So did Kuo Ch'ung-wang. He and his wife fled to another county where they found temporary employment as primary school teachers. Later they fled that school and disappeared altogether. Nobody in Long Bow heard of their whereabouts thereafter.

In Ch'ung-wang's absence, his brother and partner in business, Fu-wang, was brought before the Peasants' Association. He was beaten so severely that he died a few days later, but in spite of this violent treatment he gave no hint as to where any further wealth might be found.

Resisting change, more than 800,000 people died, according to figures issued by the Chinese government itself. Some observers believe the toll to be even higher. For centuries the gentry, although not officially part of the government, still had controlled town and village society. They had ridden out peasant uprisings, even the Taiping. They had weathered every storm, including the 1911 Revolution. Far-reaching change in China had never touched the village and the peasants. But the Communists had based their strength and future on peasant support, on their grievances against government and landlords, and their great thirst for land. Building on peasant hatred and centuries-old government suppression, Communists set out to eradicate the gentry as a class and place land in the hands of peasants. They succeeded.

Foreigners lost in China too. Their property was taken over and they were ordered out. British who had investments in China lost at least $20 million. The Japanese were even harder hit. Along with businessmen and others, foreign Christian missionaries were excluded from China too, their churches placed in the hands of Chinese priests and ministers. And as Communists under Mao Tse-tung began to suppress capitalism—private ownership and endeavor—and eliminate the gentry and return land to the peasants, they worked in other ways as well to

Room used by Mao
Tse-tung in Yenan,
Shensi province, after
the Long March.

A PICTURE PORTFOLIO: CHINA TODAY

Opposite: Heating iron in a commune factory in Canton.

The rice transplanter, a relatively new development in agriculture, is being used increasingly on Chinese farms.

A butcher cuts meat to order in a commune store in Canton.

Harnessed and straining, men tow a boat upstream on the Yangtze River.

Opposite: Farmers take a break from their work to study the writings of Mao Tse-tung.

TRAINING YOUTH FOR COMMUNISM

Communist or otherwise, whether a revolution endures depends largely on how well the young are trained to believe in and continue it. Mao Tse-tung and other Chinese leaders as well viewed education as the bedrock on which to erect a new order. They believed this simply because they considered politics the basic factor in life and education the instrument of politics.

Confucian education was moral. Its major purpose was to mold a particular kind of individual, one possessing filial piety and an attitude of obedience to authority and respect for elders. The new education in China was meant to be moral also. Its chief purpose too, beginning with children at an early age, was to produce a particular kind of individual, the socialist man or woman.

CHILD TRUST INSTITUTES

In China today the typical boy or girl becomes acquainted with the world outside the family at a much earlier age than before. Children now are brought up almost as much by society at large as they are by the family. Thousands of children between ages two and four or five attend nursery schools or, as the Chinese term in literal translation has it, "child trust institutes." As a consequence the indoctrination of children begins early and, at the same time, both parents are free to work. "Life in the nursery is, by and large, a happy one," wrote one student of Chinese society.

The young children call the nursery teacher *ku-ku* (aunt), which still carries with it the familial intimacy in which perhaps the children feel more at home. The nursery children have a great deal of activity in play as well as in work such as keeping themselves and the place clean. Group life is predominant. One often finds the nursery children in cities going to the park in groups, holding each other's hands, and guided by a nursery teacher. Right from infancy, they are brought up to the feeling that they are part of the great society and have their share in its assets and its well-being. They feel that their parents are also part of the same society and have the same share as themselves. The children feel that they belong to the public, the society, and the State more than they belong to their parents. Of course, when the parents have no opportunity in terms of possessions or in terms of authority to exercise domination over their children, the parents and children are both conscious that the only concern and authority is the State's.

KINDERGARTEN AND UPWARD

Kindergarten, which lasts through age six or seven, follows nursery school. Formerly, children at this stage in school began to master the written Chinese language and read books, carrying loads of homework away from school each day. Now Chinese kindergartens emphasize group games, handwork, singing, story telling, and sight-seeing.

There is no compulsory school attendance law in China. None is needed. The traditional Chinese respect for education carried over under the new regime. Schooling was, and is, looked upon as a privilege, not an obligation.

Consequently, now that schooling is widespread in China, most children continue their education into the primary school. Here they become acquainted with the language on a formal basis, devoting twelve out of twenty-four periods a week—or half the time—to speech and writing. According to a dictionary compiled in the seventeenth century, there were 42,174 characters in the written Chinese language. About 14,000 were of practical use. After the 1911 revolution, Chinese educators developed a list of from 1,000 to 1,200 characters necessary for literacy, although these still were written in the traditional manner. During the 1950s there was considerable discussion pro and con about language simplification. Compromise resulted. The twenty-six characters of the Latin, or English, alphabet were introduced as a supplement to written Chinese and many of the written characters themselves were simplified. The number of brush strokes required to form them was reduced. The three

characters representing Mao Tse-tung, for example, formerly consisted of four, sixteen, and eight strokes respectively. Now they can be written with four, eight, and five strokes. Mao himself, however, was probably unimpressed. Proud of his skill in calligraphy, he undoubtedly clung to the old way.

In 1964, disagreeing somewhat with the 1911 list, the government established a list of 2,328 words considered basic to knowing how to read and write. Earlier, in the 1950s, book, magazine, and newspaper publishers adopted the western style of printing characters horizontally across the page, instead of vertically, the traditional way.

Precisely what the literacy rate is today in China, which contains some 800 million people, no one knows. It can be safely assumed, though, that it is higher—probably much higher—than the 15 to 20 percent figure estimated before the Communist triumph in 1949.

Along with language simplification, there has been a strong movement to unify the spoken language to overcome differences in dialects that have persisted for centuries in China. Teachers teach in *kuo yu*—the national language—pronounced as it is in Peking. Abolishing dialectical differences in a country as vast and varied as China will be an immense task, probably progressing over decades.

Besides the language, pupils in the four-year primary schools study history, geography, some science and mathematics, and have periods of handwork, recreation, and physical education. The trend in China has been to reduce the number of courses as well as the length of formal schooling.

The emphasis in schools, beginning with the nursery schools and continuing without letup into colleges and universities, is on politics, labor, and production. These are, as observers have noted, the main themes in many textbooks on all levels.

For example, Book One of a set of primary school readers published shortly after the establishment of the new regime by the Lien Ho Publishing Company in Shanghai contains five lessons on labor and the use of the hands and six lessons on farming and vegetable planting. These themes are carried through the other books. In Book One, we find, "I have hands, you have hands, everybody has hands, everybody should use hands." Book Three says: "From the glowing east rises the sun; from China comes Mao Tse-tung; he leads us in production; with increased production, there is food and clothing and no poverty."

There are stories of labor heroes who excel in production, and many lessons are devoted to the praise of Mao Tse-tung and stories of his exemplary childhood. The army is glorified, while landlords, Chiang Kai-shek, and American imperialism are objects of derision. One book tells the story of a rich landlord who does no work all day long but enjoys good food, good clothing, and good housing and becomes fat. On a hot day he lies on a reclining chair and asks a servant to fan him. "Look," he says, "my perspiration has all disappeared." "Yes," answers the servant, "it has come to my body."

Exaltation of the Communist Party goes with the praise of Mao Tse-tung. Ideological concepts are introduced early to accompany political indoctrination. Science and nature study—birds, bugs, flowers, the sun, the wind, and so forth—are given attention because the Marxist [Communist] ideology is supposed to be scientific. Evolution is considered essential; a lesson titled "Our Ancestor" tells in an oversimplified manner how man evolved from the ape. Superstition is attacked as unscientific; so is "belief in the spirit."

Under a dictatorship, it is not uncommon to glorify the leader. Nor is it uncommon to constantly vilify those considered enemies and to try to erase attitudes which tend to make the past preferable to the present. Schools and textbooks serve as primary means of instilling new attitudes and behaviors in children and youth. Beginning at the lowest school levels, Chinese children are taught to love and glorify their leaders, and to believe in their government.

Literacy is one objective of Chinese schooling. The development of proper political thinking and insuring continued devotion to the nation are the others. Schools also exist to train cadres—essentially local leaders—in the continuing struggle to throw off the old and remold China. Individualism, which in Communist theory underlies and reinforces capitalism, is suppressed. Teachers and textbooks stress and exalt the welfare of the group, to contribute to which is the only reason for individual existence. Students receive grades in school, ranging from 1, the lowest, to 5, the highest. But these indicate an individual's progress in relation to himself, not to others. Most receive 4s and 5s. As a matter of course, no one fails. Except in athletics, competition is held to a minimum.

Students on all levels of schooling are expected not only to study, but also to perform labor for the good of society. Manual labor is a part of every school curriculum.

Primary school children clean parks, neighborhoods, and their school and grounds. Some regularly clean public buildings such as theaters. Others, during hot weather, appear at bus stops in cities to offer cold drinks of water to drivers and conductors. Older students, university students included, are expected to perform some labor in a factory or on a farm. Teachers too must work with their hands during a part of the year. The objective here is one Mao Tse-tung long held uppermost: avoid developing an educated elite like the scholar-literati of the past. Mao remained constantly on guard against the elevation of the expert to a position of prominence and importance. He preferred "red"—or proper political and social thinking and behavior—over "expert," the skilled and trained technician or professional who might wish to attain individualistic pride and self-aggrandizement from his work. This struggle has been continuous.

Boys and girls and youth work in teams formed within the Young Pioneer Brigades to which all between ages seven and fifteen belong. Brigades are broken down into companies, platoons, and squads, each with its own leader. All Young Pioneers sport proudly a red scarf around their necks, symbolizing membership.

BEYOND PRIMARY GRADES

Completing primary school at age eleven or twelve, Chinese children split up for secondary education. Some go to the general middle, or secondary school, which emphasizes academic subjects. This amounts to college preparation for many. The larger group of students goes on to technical and vocational middle schools, which in the rural areas stress agricultural education. In all middle schools families pay a small fee for their children to attend. "Peking No. 31 Middle School," an observer wrote in the 1970s,

was a missionary school before Liberation, but in 1949 it changed over to serve the workers. The teachers are paid by the State, but the school is run by a revolutionary committee of 18 members led by the Party district committee. The 18 comprise four from the workers' and soldiers' Mao Tse-tung Thought propaganda team, six of the original cadres remolded during the Cultural Revolution [in the 1960s, discussed

later], including the former headmaster and administrator, four other teachers and four students elected by the students. . . . There are 30 classes, 90 teachers, and 48 other staff—including the instructor-workers in the four school workshops (car wiring circuits; printed electronic circuits; machine tools—brake cylinders and other car or truck parts; triodes). A hundred [among the 1,600 students] at a time work in the four workshops; each pupil spends one month a year in the workshop and one month a year on a commune. They work in conjunction with local factories not just to produce goods, although of course they do, or to get income for the school, although that is also achieved, but to learn the unity of science and practice to temper their minds politically and scientifically, and to improve their physical skills. But school is not all workshops and playground; there is "academic" study too. Each day starts at 8 A.M. with a political class—most recently they had studied the Communist Manifesto. Hourly lessons are interrupted by a half-hour's physical education from 9:50–10:20. Lunch can be eaten at home or at school. After, at 2:00, there are 2 more hours of class, 2½ hours of extra-class activity, and an hour's homework to take home at 6:30. . . . There are ten basic subjects taught: politics, Chinese, mathematics, a foreign language (it was English at this school), physics, chemistry, basic agriculture, health science, history, and geography. I was particularly interested in health science, because, amongst other reasons, I had seen middle school children in Shanghai helping and receiving instruction in an urban clinic. In this they are taught anatomy and physiology, the common diseases and how to prevent and treat them, and the elements of acupuncture [treatment by the insertion of long needles into the body]—they practice on each other.

There is some instruction in sexual physiology, mainly for girls between 14 and 15, but it is not greatly emphasized. . . . By the time we reached Peking, we were no longer shy about asking questions. "I can see your school is very good," said one of our party, "but even so, 17- or 18-year-olds must play truant occasionally. What happens then?" I expected the question to be dismissed but it wasn't at all. "Well, we try reasoning—and then we go to see the family . . ." It was here that the little Red Guard girl interrupted the revolutionary committee chairman: "Oh no you don't—first of all we little Red Guards reason with him—only if we fail . . ." The Chairman agreed. "Then we go to see the family and ask: has he not a grandfather or mother, or an uncle who can tell him about the bitter past?" "And then," our questioner persisted, "if that fails, do you beat him?" There was a shocked silence —"No, we never use corporal punishment —discussion, not coercion is our method."

TO COLLEGE AND UNIVERSITY

Before the Communist victory, sixteen private missionary colleges operated in China. Three were Catholic, thirteen Protestant. There were also a number of public institutions, such as the University of Peking, maintained by the government. After 1949 the government took over the private colleges and today there are no private educational institutions in China.

University entrance is by examination, although not one based on an ability to memorize and recite Confucian wisdom as in the past. On the whole, entrance to higher education has been made easier than it once was, causing some persons worry about a general and harmful lowering of standards. In addition to displaying some academic preparation and aptitude, a university applicant must present additional qualifications, without which no amount of academic ability will help. He or she must come from a family that possesses no record of being anti-government. Further, the applicant must display "progressiveness" in his thinking, and he must have demonstrated political reliability in the past. An applicant must be a member of the Communist Youth League or at least be free from any objection by the League. Finally, he must be recommended by an official of the factory, commune, or army unit of which he is a member.

University education in China is still for the few, and it leads to a position in the professions, in industry, or in government. But university education, like all other in China, is grounded on labor and production. Speaking of Tsinghua Technical University in Peking, composed of seven thousand teachers, students, and staff concentrating on electronics, mechanical engineering, and mechanics, an observer wrote:

No longer do students come, after examinations, direct from middle schools. They come from production to learn to go back to production. The masses in the localities are asked to nominate suitable people who have worked for two or three years at least. There are normally five conditions that must be fulfilled (although some veteran factory floor workers are recruited). They must be adept in the living study and application of Marxism-Leninism-Mao Tse-tung Thought; have close links with the masses; have practical experience; have been at middle school at least until 16; and be 20 years old. They stay for two or three years with all expenses paid. Veteran workers continue to receive their wages.

Once at Tsinghua students study theory and practice of production, often on the actual site. The university, in fact, incorporates a motor vehicle plant, a provision factory, and an electronic works. Their main purpose is to combine with other teaching facilities, but they also produced 2.7 million yuans' [one yuan is about 40 cents] worth of goods in 1970. They do not provide the only practical facilities. The original laboratories have been improved and carry out research work asked for by the State. The university runs an experimental farm in Kiangsi Province, which, as well as providing opportunities for productive labor and experimental material on how a socialist university can serve agriculture, produced 2.8 million catties [one catty is equivalent to 1.1 pounds] of grain. Some teaching and research is done on construction sites (dams, bridges, chemical engineering) throughout China. The university

Children reading rented comic books in Peking. Although some of the books contain traditional folk tales, most are patriotic stories about the deeds of revolutionary heroes.

organizes training courses in factories and communes on how to do research. They organize teachers and students to study society to summarize the advances made by peasants, workers and students, and put them into the textbooks. Thus they have broken down the conventions which separate university and society to their mutual benefit. There are no examinations as we know them in the West—but mutual checks and assessment of their progress with the help of each other and textbooks. One veteran worker at Tsinghua related his experiences:

"After six months we have put our experience into theory, and transformed the theories we have been taught into practice. In the process of teaching we use Chairman Mao's principle: officers teach soldiers, soldiers teach officers, all teach each other. Students give lectures as well as do practical work. I went on to the platform and lectured on technical innovation, on advanced experience in our factory and how productivity has been raised. The other students said I was easy to understand because I spoke in workers' language.

"This is the revolution in proletarian education, new in world history. We learn as we go on how to follow Chairman Mao's revolutionary road."

Teachers in lower schools earn from forty to one hundred *renminpi* ("people's currency," formerly yuan) a month, depending on experience and responsibilities. University teachers start at around one hundred renminpi a month, and some earn as much as two hundred renminpi a month. Chinese teachers on the whole work hard for their money, and they occupy positions of respect, as teachers always have in China. On all levels teachers are constantly scrutinized by students, members of the Communist Youth League, administrators, and each other. They frequently engage in group and self-criticism. Teachers in China can seldom slide by with lack of class preparation or enthusiasm, or with the sloppy examination and grading of student work.

Few aspects of Chinese culture have changed more deeply, rapidly, and constantly than education. Length of schooling has been altered from time to time. So has the number of courses. In some instances, peasant groups have established schools without much reference to governmental authority, although sticking with Mao's thought essentially. Education in China remains in a state of flux.

Chairman Mao himself suggested from time to time that reading books could get to be too much of a good thing. A person could overdo it. Mao, more than anyone, kept educational emphasis on labor and production, on practical, not simply academic, activity. When students were criticized for falling asleep in class, Mao replied that sleep was better for them than listening to boring lectures. He blamed teachers, implying that they should change their ways. Mao favored shortening courses of study and time spent in school.

Above all, schools remain political. "The workers' propaganda teams should stay permanently in the schools and take part in fulfilling all the tasks of struggle-criticism-transformation in the schools, and they will always lead the schools," said Mao. And at another time: "Students, while taking studies as the main task, should learn other things as well, namely, besides learning literature they must also learn industry, agriculture, and military science, and they must also criticize the bourgeoisie" [the capitalist middle class].

Schools everywhere exist to insure the continuation of a society's culture, instilling and maintaining the values most members of a society prize. This is particularly true in China, where the purpose of schools remains to help reinforce and continue a Communist society, to produce succeeding generations of the socialized individual.

CHANGES IN MARRIAGE AND RELIGION

Partly because of more years spent on education, partly owing to the emphasis on labor and production, Chinese couples today tend to marry later in life than once was the case. In older times, a girl of twenty who was not married and producing children caused parents grave concern. A man of twenty-five and still unmarried was shirking filial duties, and the clan and the community let him know that. All this has changed. Women tend to wait until their mid-twenties before marrying, men even longer, and the government encourages that.

More frequently than not, marriages in China today are arranged by the couples involved, rather than by their families as in the past. Although accelerated under Communist rule, this trend was not entirely new. Following the Revolution of 1911, particularly in cities, young men and women began a movement away from family-arranged marriages. This, however, did not spread into the countryside where tradition remained firm and persistent. Nor, for that matter, did marriage based on love and free choice become widespread in cities outside educated and sophisticated circles.

Once in power, Mao's government gave almost immediate attention to marriage, issuing a law in 1950 that called for the abolition of old ways. According to the government when it issued the new law, there would be no more marriage without the couple's free choice and consent, no more "body price" or gifts, no more child brides, no more mother-in-law domination. According to those who favored it, this law marked the first step toward dismantling a social structure that had for centuries chained women to "the bottom rung of the ladder in a ten-thousand-foot well of sorrow."

THE NEW ROLE OF WOMEN

Students of China had noted that the authority of the husband had been weakening for some time. This had particularly been the case among poor peasants, where out of economic necessity women had had to perform much manual labor if the family were to survive. Because of their value, such women enjoyed a considerable voice in family affairs. The contrary was true, of course, among the richer classes, where women contributed much less economically.

At one time it had been common in China to bind women's feet, especially among the middle and upper classes. Toes and heels were drawn toward each other, the foot firmly wrapped. Small feet were considered a mark of feminine beauty, but binding brought terrible deformity. Footbinding was outlawed after the 1911 revolution, and the practice finally disappeared. Today in China there are no classes, officially, and all women, according to their ability, are expected to perform the same kind of labor as men.

To observers of China today, the contrast between the old and the new with respect to women appears especially striking. Women seem to enjoy more freedom than in the past.

CHANGE COMES SLOWLY

In some respects, change in women's status has been slow and remains incomplete. A visitor to China in the 1970s found only one woman on the seven-member revolutionary committee at an electric motor plant. When questioned, the woman carefully contrasted the situation with conditions in the past, a not uncommon way to explain things when defending a new society and the practices that go with it.

Forty-one-year-old Han Ai-hua expressed surprise when I said women's representation on this leading body wasn't quite up to many people's idea of women's equality.

When she cited the "heavier than men's oppression" of women before 1949 and that now they get the same pay for the same work, I told her I knew this. But, I said, this wouldn't satisfy women's liberation advocates in the United States.

Her reply was: "Getting rid of some of the attitudes ingrained in men and women in a nation as old as China isn't easy." She said I should remember that women 35 years old and up had had far less education than men. Assuring me women in their 20s were on their way up, Han Ai-hua told me

there were 6 women among the 15 group leaders in the plant. She also pointed out that Chinese women keep their maiden names after marriage.

In marriage the emphasis officially, and to a large extent in practice, is on the couple, not on the family's interest and welfare. The influence and authority of age have been weakened. The importance of clan, ancestors, and family line has diminished.

From the family, emphasis has shifted to the individual, which runs directly counter to tradition. This does not mean, however, that the Chinese government has erected individualism in the western sense as an ideal. Far from it. Ultimate loyalty is now directed to the nation, to society, to the people as a whole. And perhaps nothing better illustrates the extensive change that has taken place in this regard since 1949 than the following story and comment by two observers who lived for a time in Peking:

The Summer Palace on the outskirts of Peking, the luxurious folly of the last Empress Dowager, who built it with monies allocated for an imperial navy, is now a popular playground. In summer the huge lake, with its arched marble bridges, is alive with swimmers and rowers, and in winter its precarious icy surface swarms with skaters. Inevitably, as on all natural lakes used for skating, there are a few accidents. The remarkable aspect of one much-publicized accident was not that a young man fell through the ice and was rescued, but that literally dozens of skaters and bystanders rushed to his aid and in the process also went through the thin ice. All were saved by helping one another and attributed their survival to the thought of Chairman Mao.

What was the meaning of this rather strange incident? Would it not have been more sensible, we asked our Chinese friends, for one or two people, preferably expert swimmers, to take the responsibility for the rescue rather than run the risk of an unnecessary mass tragedy? To view the matter in such a way, they told us, was to miss the whole point. In the old society, no one would have attempted to save the victim of an accident. One's responsibilities were to his own family. Who would care for them if one should drown trying to help a stranger? The remarkable thing about the incident described was that many people had so changed their world outlook that they had reflexively acted to save an unknown person.

Americans would recognize altruistic behavior—unselfishly helping even a total stranger—as common to their culture. It has not, however, been common to oriental cultures. Perhaps it is becoming so in China although, of course, one example does not necessarily mean that all Chinese uphold altruism today.

GRATITUDE TO THE STATE

Chinese are expected to be grateful for jobs, and so on, to the Party, the government, especially the leader. It became common to hear a person express gratitude by saying, "I have Chairman Mao to thank for this."

During the early years of the Communist regime especially, young people were encouraged to report wrongdoing by their parents and other elders, such as tax evasion, bribery, theft, cheating on contracts with the government, and the like. And confessions were extracted from a good many alleged lawbreakers as a result of young people's activities in schools, in factories and on farms, and in homes. Confucius once was asked, "Should the son serve as witness against the father who has stolen a sheep?" Confucius replied, "The

son shields the father and the father shields the son." Such an attitude is now considered reactionary and antisocial, although this is not to say that Confucian principles and ideals are entirely gone from China.

From the beginning the new Chinese government gave a great deal of attention to stamping out ancestor veneration. The five Confucian relationships were dismissed as nonsense. Only one relationship mattered—that of the individual to his group and by extension to his government and nation.

DECLINE OF THE GODS

As has been the case in all cultures, attention to the supernatural among the Chinese, peasants in particular, stemmed from the need for confidence and strength in the face of insurmountable natural forces. Consequently worship of the gods of flood, the Dragon God which controlled water and rain, the gods of earth and grain, and others, naturally followed. The kinship system, along with agricultural production and the agrarian life, led to the development of ancestor veneration to perpetuate the economy and the social system.

From the peasant's point of view, success depended not so much on his own efforts and achievements as on the favor and good fortune the gods bestowed. In time of trouble he tended to try to appease the appropriate deity through worship and sacrifice, hoping for easement. Or he might indulge in an appropriate rite or ceremony dictated by a more or less organized religion such as Taoism or Buddhism. The peasant was, however, at the same time realistic. He believed that self-help was as important as prayer and ceremony. "Do the utmost within human power, but accept the ordinance of Heaven," became his guide.

Even before the advent of Communism an antireligion movement developed in China, resulting largely from the 1911 revolution.

Communists, however, were especially committed to an antireligious attitude, upholding as they did Marxist atheism and materialism. The Chinese constitution of 1953, handed down by the Communist government, guaranteed "freedom of religious belief," whatever that might be interpreted to mean. And, while there were sporadic outbreaks of violent antireligious activity, the guarantee, so far as anyone can tell, has been honored. Chinese peasants clung for centuries to age-old and comforting religious beliefs, and they were at the same time highly superstitious. Not even Communists believe that change will take place in China overnight.

Perhaps if material life improves, peasants will shed religious beliefs. Yet no one can say that they have been eliminated today from Chinese life. In time of flood a peasant might well pray to the old gods for relief. At the same time he will hope that government engineers and relief in the way of food and clothing are at hand. He might pray that sickness not take a child from him. He also hopes that a doctor or a paramedic will arrive at his house in time. If there is drought, prayer might help. But the government's ability to quickly allocate grain and buy grain if necessary from other countries might be beneficial too.

The government has, on the whole, tended to move religion almost exclusively into the family. It has de-emphasized the institutional side—temples and priests of whatever faith.

Most important of all, there are the young, receiving a new and state-oriented education. Upon coming to power Mao dismissed those over thirty years of age from his attention. He concentrated on educating youth. How extensively this will affect religion in China is uncertain. It seems unlikely, however, that the new education will have no effect at all.

What of Buddhism, that great religion which swept China in the centuries following the downfall of the Han Dynasty? Buddhism's status is difficult to determine. Many temples have been closed, monks and nuns scattered. In Tibet, west of China proper, Buddhism is for all purposes the national religion. China assumed direct control of Tibet, over which it had exercised indirect control for centuries, in the 1950s. Apparently, insofar as it has not served as a nucleus or rallying point for anti-Chinese government activity, Buddhism has gone unmolested in Tibet.

In northwest China there are perhaps as many as ten million Muslims, followers of Islam, the way of Allah. Muslims have inhabited the area for centuries. Islam, begun by Muhammad in Arabia in the seventh century A.D., is also the religion of peoples of such Arabian countries as Syria and Saudi Arabia, as well as of peoples of Egypt, Turkey, Indonesia, and Pakistan. The Chinese government has enjoyed friendly relations with these countries. It has done little to hamper Muslim religious practices in China. The government does not consider Islam "imperialistic." That is, Islam is not a religion whose followers would be inclined to try to bring down the Communist regime.

Not so Christianity. Christianity was a religion supported by western nations. Predominantly Christian nations like the United States bitterly opposed Communism and the new regime.

In 1948, according to Catholic sources, China contained about 3.3 million Catholic Christians. The Church operated 3 universities, 189 secondary schools, 1,500 city primary and 2,243 village primary schools, as well as over 200 hospitals and 200 orphanages. These and other church-operated social institutions were useful to the government. Their operation, as well as that of similar institutions run by Protestants, was allowed to continue. The government, however, would not allow any religious body to participate in political activity. Going even further than this, the government ordered all foreign missionaries from the country. All connections between Chinese Christians and churches in the United States and elsewhere were severed. Said Chou En-lai, for a time premier of China, to Chinese Christian leaders:

> So we are going to let you go on teaching, go on trying to convert the people, provided you also continue your social services. After all, we both believe that truth will prevail; we think your beliefs untrue and false, therefore if we are right, the people will reject them, and your church will decay. If you are right, then the people will believe you; but as we are sure that you are wrong, we are prepared for that risk.

Later the government modified its policy concerning foreign missionaries. It offered to admit them on a one-to-one basis from any country that would, in turn, allow Chinese missionaries—that is, Communist propagandists—to work in it. So far as anyone knows, there were no takers.

Little is known about the actual state of Christianity in China today. It was never a strong religious force in China and, in all likelihood, especially among the young, its influence has considerably diminished. And as the Chinese government provided more and more social services such as medical care and education, those offered by Christian churches lessened in importance.

In the 1970s, on the other hand, Confucianism and ancestor veneration appeared to retain some strength. In the spring of 1974, at any rate, nearly thirty years after Communist victory, the government launched another strong campaign against Confucius. Articles condemning Confucius appeared in magazines and newspapers, and local government officials were encouraged to attack him and his ideas. Among other things, writers accused Confucius of upholding and reinforcing the "slave system" of upper class exploitation and rule over the workers. It is true that Confucianism, emphasizing obedience and filial piety, proved a handy instrument for perpetuating landlord and upper class domination. When one speaks of past Chinese civilization one refers to upper class culture, not that of the majority of the people. But this has been the case with all past societies. The majority of the world's population, until fairly recently, was composed of illiterate peasants whose attitudes and lives changed little over the centuries.

LABOR AND PRODUCTION IN THE FACTORIES

"I am coming back," wrote a Chinese capitalist and factory owner from Hong Kong, to which he had fled following Communist victory in 1949, "not because I expect that I shall be allowed to make a fortune out of my business, but because I am told that as I was not a hard employer the Communists have no complaint against me. I shall be able to make a living, my work interests me, and although my son will never be allowed to inherit the business, he is a good engineer and will always be acceptable as a technical expert."

Not all Chinese capitalists—factory and business owners—felt this way by any means. A good many of them—no one knows how many thousands—taking what assets they could with them, left China and stayed away. Those who remained, or returned, were subject to numerous restrictions. They no longer could produce what they pleased, but only what and how much the government required. Most, perhaps all, capitalists were subjected to "reeducation." They were required to attend classes to master Chinese Communist theory and doctrine. Further, they were expected to conduct themselves always in accord with that doctrine. Managers were required not only to manage, but also to perform physical labor, an hour or two each week at least. Even high-level managers had to spend at least one month a year in physical labor. And managers were, of course, expected to fulfill government-assigned production quotas.

Industry scarcely existed in China before the 1950s, and even now China must still be classified as largely an agricultural nation. Previously a few large iron and steel mills and textile plants could be found in such cities as Shanghai. Most were destroyed by war. The bulk of China's industrial production was accomplished by small factories and shops, many of which remain in operation at the present time. The state of China's industrial economy today is not clear, for the government releases few statistics on production. There is no doubt, however, that China has made considerable progress in developing industry and that it is making ever-increasing use of its vast resources of coal, iron ore, oil, and other minerals such as antimony and tungsten.

Upon gaining power in 1949, the Communist government proceeded to nationalize—that is, change from private to public ownership—all industry and business. This did not occur overnight. Although it was a gradual process, it was at the same time inexorable. Figures gleaned from here and there tell at least a part of the story.

In 1949 there appear to have been some

Opposite: A worker reads the latest factory news. Hung on a line like laundry, it describes the accomplishments of individual work brigades and exhorts workers on to even greater achievements.

123,000 privately owned industrial establishments. This number rose to 150,000 in 1952—for reasons not entirely clear—and then fell to 89,000 in 1956. One year later the number was about a thousand. Employment in private industry dropped from 1.6 million in 1949 to 14,000 in 1956.

Primary targets for nationalization were industries and businesses owned and operated by such wealthy families as the Soongs and the Chiangs. From there the government moved on to take over smaller firms. The process accelerated in the 1950s during the "Five-Antis" campaign—against bribery of public officials, fraud in government contracts, tax evasion, theft of state-owned assets, and misuse or betrayal of state economic assets. Thousands of businesses were investigated and offenders found guilty were fined or imprisoned. Many firms were taken over by the government. Those who lost their property were paid for it, in many cases token amounts, not what they thought their business or industry was worth. In numerous instances a combination of government-private ownership resulted, with owners retaining a voice in an industry subject to extensive governmental regulation, taxation, and production quotas.

In China today industrial as well as agricultural production is closely regulated. In the beginning the government needed capitalists' knowledge and experience. It could not have done without them, although Communist leaders believed that in the not distant future capitalists themselves no longer would be necessary. Capitalists consequently were not immediately eliminated as a class, as landlords were. But those who chose to accept the new regime in many instances underwent direct, intensive, and sometimes harsh reeducation to remold their ideas.

It is difficult for observers from such capitalistic nations as the United States to believe that a society in which there is no distinction between workers and managers and no real money incentive to produce can long prevail without severe damage to the economy. They may be right. On the other hand, extensive change has occurred in China, and the future remains difficult to predict.

WORKERS UNIONIZED

There are trade unions in China, with membership numbering over twenty million. Union leaders are chiefly concerned with acting as channels of information between the Communist Party and workers. Within factories union committees concern themselves with social welfare activities—medical and educational services, and so on. Their duties also include mobilizing and motivating workers to achieve ever greater production goals. Workers' right to strike is guaranteed by the Chinese Constitution, although in a situation where the people own the means of production, to create a work stoppage would mean that workers were striking against themselves.

Chinese factories, especially large ones, provide much more than regular employment and monthly wages. They offer educational resources such as nursery schools and adult education classes. Many of them operate dormitories for workers and provide meals. Nearly all offer medical services for employees, and in large factories, hospital care as well. Utilizing doctors, nurses, and paramedics—"barefoot doctors"—of all kinds, the government has practically wiped out cholera, smallpox, venereal disease, typhoid, and typhus, which in the past killed millions annually. This has been a signal achievement. The government also has made great strides in controlling hookworm, dysentery, tuberculosis, and malaria. These also formerly reaped a huge annual harvest of life in China, as inevitable as flood, drought, and famine.

As in agriculture, extensive planning is central to China's industrial economy. Government plans, commonly called Five-Year Plans, dictate what and how much is produced in Chinese industry. These plans are not, however, made without reference to committees within the Communist Party responsible for management. Nor are they developed without some regard for workers within an industry. How many tons of iron and steel this year? How many pairs of shoes or pants? How many nuts and bolts? What resources for production can be counted on? What transportation facilities can be depended on? How will industrial production as a whole be coordinated? And how will the goods produced be allocated and distributed among consumers? In China numerous governmental committees on several levels concern themselves with these problems. The whole business of national planning is very complex, with the possibility of error compounded by the host of goods to be produced and distributed and the more than 100,000 individual enterprises producing them. On more than one occasion serious planning mistakes have occurred.

AT WORK AND AT HOME

Many China observers tend to be sympathetic to the new regime. Consequently their reports might lack balance. Still, even allowing for bias, reports can be useful to gain some ideas about factory life in China today. For example, a problem concerning quality arose in a bicycle factory:

The Second Bicycle Factory in Tientsin received many complaints from customers that its product was too slow and heavy. The plant decided to replace scattered steel balls in the middle shaft by ball brackets to make the bike easier to ride, but it seemed that this would increase the cost by 3.5 cents in Chinese currency (an amount equal to 1 cent in other currencies). Could this quality improvement be accomplished without increasing the cost? There appeared to be a contradiction between cost and quality. But through an analytic struggle the plant aimed to carry out the "general line" of "greater, faster, better, and cheaper."

The enterprise party committee made this problem a subject of mass discussion and analysis. All personnel attended various meetings and many formed problem-solving teams consisting of managers, technicians, and workers. Employees submitted more than three hundred "innovation" measures for practicing economy, with the aim of saving 3.6 cents instead of increasing the cost of the bike by 3.5 cents. Many innovations were introduced, the quality was improved, and in a few months unit cost decreased by 50 cents. . . .

A report from the Shenyang Transformer Factory deals with another important aspect of workers' lives—their wages:

In general, wages range from a low for "grade one" of about 33 yuan a month to a high for "grade eight" of around 100 yuan. In a few cases beginning workers get less than 30 yuan and sometimes technicians, engineers, or veteran cadres get over 100 yuan a month. The average wage at most factories we visited was between 40 and 50 yuan a month.

These figures are low by U.S. standards. But in terms of "real wages"—what can be bought with that money—they are not all that low. Rent is low (usually 5 percent of a family's income), food is very cheap, medical care is free or at nominal cost, pensions are guaranteed, and there are no [income] taxes. We asked several families to outline their monthly budget. Everyone had plenty to cover the basics of shelter, heat, and food; they had money for entertainment and other sundries and they usually had made purchases of items like children's toys, clothing, and other daily needs. Most families also owned consumer items like bicycles, radios, wrist watches, and sewing machines. These take up a higher percentage of wages than do the basic necessities of life. For example, a bicycle or sewing machine costs a little over two months' average salary. Everyone also had money left over to save; in some families this came to 30–40 percent of their total monthly income. It was clear that real wages in China allow for a very adequate standard of living; a "simple" standard, compared to U.S. life, but one that has risen over the years and shows every promise of continuing to rise. Compared to conditions of old China the differences are, as we were told, "like comparing night and day." . . .

A visitor to China reported on family life and activities after working hours among Chinese city dwellers:

Here is an apartment block at a "New Workers Village," in a textile-mill district of Shanghai. We knock on doors and talk with those we find at home. It is 4:00 P.M., and those on day shift are still at work. Children play noisily under the spreading plane trees which shade the space between blocks. A group of neighbors sit fanning themselves, talking about prices, drinking tea. Mrs. Tan is at home with her son, who is back from Anhwei province for a month to see the family. He was sent there for practical work after finishing Middle School. The family of five has two rooms, plus a kitchen shared with two other families. Father earns 72 renminpi per month, mother 58 renminpi (a pension, three quarters of her wage before retirement). Rent is 5 renminpi per month. Another son, graduate of Communications University at Sian, works in a mining-machine factory in remote Tsinghai province. A third is on a state farm not far away, earning only 24 renminpi a month. Furnishings are of the simplest. But the beds, mosquito-netted and covered with *tatami* [woven mats], are comfortable. There is a radio and a bicycle. Mrs. Tan is saving to buy a sewing machine, which will cost her F150. [F means *fen,* an amount equal to about 1 cent.] Food for each person costs about F15 per month. Meat is not cheap; F65 for a kilo of salted pork. Only grain products are presently rationed [1971].

The Tans' conditions of life are fairly typical. Communal provision in the Workers Village is cheap and above the standard of private provision. Medical care costs Y1 per person per year. Many go twice a week to the cinema—at tiny cost. TV is available, with two and a half hours of programs each day, only at the factory; no worker has his own set. "Pure entertainment" put on by advertisers does not exist. Drama, political commentary, documentary —these are the staple, and technically they are quite well done. TV has little hold over people, and I often found myself—perhaps in a hotel lounge—the only person watching a program. People in China *talk*—endlessly, over tea, through long meals—at times when Westerners might watch TV or dress up and go out to organized entertainment. Nevertheless, the government is pushing ahead with experimental development of color TV. . . .

Many of the dozen shows I saw at theaters in China were opera-ballets. These standard eight works reflect the norm and the sum total of theater in the period since the Cultural Revolution swept "bourgeois relics" from the stage. The most popular of them is *White-haired Girl,* a tale of awful suffering and breathtaking heroism during the anti-Japanese war. I saw it in Sian. Like the other opera-ballets, it is heavily political. In its construction, however, the old is blended with the new, and the foreign with the Chinese. . . .

Theater reigns supreme in the world of Chinese entertainment. The cinema is important—yearly cinema attendance in China is at least 4 billion—but it relies heavily on the theater. There are films of the eight opera-ballets which are based squarely on the theater productions. Some 500 million patrons are said to have seen the film of *Red Detachment of Women.* . . .

AN ACCOUNT OF PROGRESS

The Chinese government's industrial objective has been to attain as high a degree of self-sufficiency as possible. Much heavy equipment was imported—such as diesel locomotives from France—but in time China had its own Shanghai Diesel Pumps and Motors Plant and similar factories.

Statistics on China's industrial production are difficult to obtain. Over the years little statistical data came out of China. Piecing together bits of information, foreign economists have derived what essentially are estimates of China's industrial growth. One such estimate concluded that, taking 1952 as 100, by the end of the 1950s production had progressed along these lines:

Electric power	571.6
Coal	391.0
Ferrous metals	765.8
Petroleum	848.6
Chemical processing	615.0
Textiles	242.3

Economists guessed that total growth in 1971 might be between 15 and 20 percent.

Chinese shipyards have produced a number of ocean-going vessels of ten thousand tons. China has developed electronic computers of various kinds. It produces automobiles, one sedan resembling a Fiat, weighing a half ton, and consuming only 1.25 gallons of gasoline every sixty-two miles. The Shanghai Heavy Machine Building Plant contains a twelve thousand ton hydraulic free-forging press, largest in the world, used for producing steel rolling mill machinery, power shafts, and large generators. Each spring and autumn the Chinese government displays a growing list of products at the trade fairs in Canton, seeking foreign buyers. And each year the number of contracts for various exports increases.

Compared to such industrial giants as the United States and the Soviet Union, China lags rather far behind. In the absence of sound statistics, one must rely for impressions on reports by foreign observers. Some of them harbor doubts about the absence of monetary motivation. Some deplore reeducation and leader-glorification, and others stress errors in planning. Most, though, seem to agree that on the whole China is better off industrially than it was before 1949. The Chinese worker is regimented. But even so, many observers appear to believe that he is better off now than in the past. China has a long way to go industrially. It continues to build. What the future holds for China as an industrial nation is, of course, impossible to predict.

LABOR AND PRODUCTION ON THE FARMS

Change has been as extensive in the Chinese countryside as in urban areas. In the beginning the new Chinese government parceled out land to peasants, granting ownership to both husband and wife, a departure from past practice. This situation was not to endure, however. The government aimed at eventual collectivization—the land owned and worked by everyone in common.

In the early 1950s, under the leadership of rural cadres, mutual aid teams were organized for farm production. The next step was to form cooperatives, many containing 150 or more families. Finally came full-scale collectivization. Rural areas were organized into communes, some containing more than 4,000 families and 50,000 people. These economic, social, and political units are collectively operated by the people who live in them. The communal goal is socialistic, cooperative production, officially at least for the good of everyone. And each commune supports schools, factories, frequently a hospital, and cultural institutions such as theaters.

By the late 1960s there were some 70,000 communes in China. Altogether they held about 100 million families, probably between 500 and 600 million people, about the entire Chinese agricultural population. A visitor in the 1970s described communes in Hsinchou County, up the Yangtze River from Wuhan. Here was an area of some 673,000 people which, at least according to the visitor, in 1971 produced 22,000 tons of grain, 13,500 tons of cotton, and thousands of pigs.

One of the outstanding successes in Hsinchou has been in its mechanization. We drove out of the county center one morning and paid a visit to the Liuchieh Commune, where in a big, spacious compound surrounded by new, red brick workshops 136 commune workers turned out necessities for the six brigades the commune is composed of. A tall, very energetic middle-aged man, Cheng Ching-chich, was obviously the moving spark in this and other commune enterprises around. Swift speaking and decisive, he is a natural leader type. The machine shop, with a history of twelve years now, has used 1,300,000 yuan in its establishment, 98 percent of the money coming from commune reserve funds. It not only produces agricultural implements for commune use, but also carries out tractor repairs, as well as doing experimentation in creating or changing implements for new tasks. We watched while a new model of rice transplanter was being tried, knowing well that this implement which has been

---

Opposite: Seated in their home are the Changs of Red Pepper Village, a commune in Hopei province.

made in so many parts of the country, tried out ever since 1958, is coming closer to the liking of commune folk than it has yet been. Despite the drawbacks each model still has in one way or another, the problems of mastering them will surely be solved. From the machine shops we went on to the commune brick works. Three hundred workers work in this large-scale plant, one hundred of whom are middle school girls who have come to communes to seek further education through practice.

The next commune factory visited was a food-processing one, which included a flour mill, an oil press, the making of dried noodles, and so on. . . .

We stopped a while with research workers of one production team, and met their leader, an ageing farmer, with a quizzical expression on his face, big eyes, and a friendly smile. "Yes," he said, pointing to a field of barley and wheat with rows interspersed, "it will probably be a very good crop this year. We have been working on seed selection, fertilizers and pesticides, and perhaps we can show more results this coming season. Yes, that is the new kind of light tube we use now for dealing with moths and such. The current that runs through the wires on each side kills the insects. It is very effective." We had seen this assembly being put together in the machine shops, where seventy had already been made for this season, with 270 more which had been ordered still to be done. . . .

It was raining lightly when we arrived at the Lienmeng Brigade of the Lienmeng Commune. . . . The brigade had its offices and some of its industrial work in the big compound of the chief local landlord, now happily forgotten. A total of 395 families make up 1,857 people who farm 21.7 hectares [a hectare: 2.471 acres] of rice paddy and 42.7 hectares of wheat fields.

The main crop is cotton. The land was once covered with sand dunes, which now are being carted away each winter when there is time enough for such work. They are first planted with a grass which grows tall, something like timothy, which is called "black wheat" here. This not only settles the sand, but can be used for fodder.

We looked over the various workshops, machine repair, grain processing, bamboo basket making, tailoring, oil pressing, cotton ginning, cotton carding, and so on, then watched seed selection, and afterwards the mass of the membership engaged in making the pressed earth cores for growing cotton seeds in. Here the process was different from that of Liuchieh, where a spade-like machine was used, but the people here thought theirs to be better. An endless container like a small cocoa tin with the bottom knocked out is made, the earth filled and hammered in with a hammer beating a wooden plug. It takes two and a half days for a worker to do as much as the Liuchieh does in one day, however.

We paid a visit to the Hsinchou county hospital, finding it to be one of 160 beds, and a staff of 132, 96 of whom are medical. There are 31 doctors, 26 of whom are graduates of universities, the other five having come up from practical work. There are 8 traditional medical practitioners including the acupuncturists. Out-patients average 300 a day. The hospital helps in training for commune hospitals and commune brigade clinics, and makes up its own herbal medicines. The county also has a 50-bed hospital for schistosomiasis, a tropical disease, which disease, however, is no longer the problem it once was, having been eliminated in the main. We visited the operating theater and watched an operation on a woman for thyroid gland trouble, acupuncture anaesthesia being used. She was quite conscious, and when asked, replied quite calmly that she felt no pain. The needle was in her wrist and was being twirled by a nurse during the process. . . .

Moving toward and achieving widespread rural collectivization, the government has altered course from time to time, officials learning as they went along. During agricultural cooperative days, for example, it was discovered that common responsibility for flocks of sheep had shortcomings. What was everyone's business became no one's business. Flocks diminished in size. Consequently, owners were made responsible for their own sheep. The sheep grew fat and the size of flocks increased. Members of communes at first were expected to take their meals together in huge mess-halls. This did not please many people. Consequently all means of coercion to achieve mass dining were dropped. Further, under the commune system, it was discovered that people put forth more effort for the good of all if at the same time they could have their own small plots of land to work. Those who wish it now have a *mou* [one sixth of an acre] or so, and may keep or sell the produce.

A COUNTRY VILLAGE

The village of Liu Ling, visited by the Swedish writer Jan Myrdal in the 1960s, is part of a commune in Shensi province, among the loess-covered hills of northern China where many people live in cave homes. A man Myrdal called the Old Secretary, Communist Party leader of Liu Ling, told him:

When I came here twenty-five years ago, only the valley was cultivated. All the fields you see up there on the hillside have been cleared since then. It is good soil down there in the valley. It yields ten times as much as that on the slopes. Down there we are able to use a tractor. We hire one from the tractor station at Yenan. We have only a couple of hundred mou which can be tilled by tractor, but the Liu Ling People's Commune has plans to buy one and a couple of trucks. But that cannot be done till the commune has made a bit more out of its factory for agricultural machinery. It's only on the actual floor of the valley that there is any tractor land.

Every member of the labor brigade is given a private plot down there. We reckon 0.4 mou per head, and everyone is included, even infants. . . . We can tell that the plots are private from the way they are all such bits and pieces. It is good land, but not really right for tractors. We try to keep the private plots separate from land we are going to use the tractor on. . . .

Up here on the hillside is where we cleared the new ground, and are still clearing. You can see that the fields are of different shapes. The big ones are collective ones. They are worked by the labor groups. . . .

Thirty-five year old Tung Wang-chen had been born in Liu Ling. Forced to serve in the Kuomintang Army during the civil war, he deserted. Said he:

There are no mornings when we sleep in. We don't do that in this part of the country. In the busiest time, harvest-time, we don't take our days off. We save them up till later in the year. No, I don't normally go and visit our neighbors in the village. After all, I see them out in the fields every day, so I don't need to visit them in the evenings as well.

It's in the winter that we rest. We collect fuel then. Either sticks and dry wood that we find, or we hack up a little coal. Actually, the children are supposed to sweep in front of the cave but they do it badly and skimp if they can. When I see that, I do it myself. We bought a bicycle in 1960, and we bought a two-wheeled cart with rubber tires in 1961. I had been thinking of buying a bicycle for a long time. It is easier to get into town if you have a bicycle. I ride the bicycle. My wife could not bicycle when we bought it. I have tried to teach her, but she still can't get on without help. . . .

I bicycle into Yenan twice a month. Then I go to the opera. If there is a good opera in Yenan, we stop work at half past five. Perhaps we decide that the whole team will go to the opera. We ride in on seven or eight bicycles, each of us taking a passenger. I usually ride in with the other men, but now and again I take my wife and the children. Mostly she does not want to come. She wants to stay with our youngest. She won't take the child to the opera. It's such a business. The older children like films best. None of us like song-and-dance. But when there's a film in the village, even Granny goes to it. . . .

A DIFFERENT WAY OF LIVING

China's Turfan Basin in the arid far northwest has been called "the Land of Fire" and "the Great Wind Pass." Here in this very dry region is located the Five Star People's Commune, population twenty-eight thousand. Over the years, according to reports, the commune's residents have planted trees as shelter belts against the strong prevailing winds and constructed irrigation works. Grapes, cotton, and grain are the commune's principal crops, although some other fruits besides grapes are grown too.

One interesting feature about this commune is that, despite government efforts to deemphasize it, the extended family appears to persist. At least this was the case with one sixty-year-old commune member named Abuliz, as reported in the 1970s. Abuliz had

married after Communists took over China in 1949. Later, three generations of his family lived together. He, his son, and his daughter-in-law worked on a farm production team. His wife occupied herself exclusively with household chores. One daughter was in a primary school, while another attended a middle school. Reportedly, in one year the family realized a thousand renminpi—about $500—as their share of communal income from grapes, fruit, and melons. With this money the family purchased blankets, quilts, clothing, two transistor radios, a bicycle, and an inexpensive sewing machine. By western standards the Abuliz family would not seem well off by any means. Five hundred dollars is not a huge annual income. By their own standards, however, they appeared to be satisfied with their lot.

In China, as is probably true most everywhere, the more people have the more they seem to want. In any event, this appears to be the case among some Chinese who at least think they are better off than they were before. One resident of Lui Ling village, Lo Han-hong, expressed the idea this way: "People live better than they used to and they are beginning to have new needs. . . . There are more and more bicycles all the time. And those who have carts and bicycles are now wanting to have radios and alarm clocks. There is no limit to their needs. The better life is, the greater becomes one's requirements." Whether a Communist society will satisfy those expanding needs remains, of course, a matter to be seen.

At the present time, according to reports, farm workers, like those in factories, receive incomes. These vary as the income of each commune varies. And this depends on crops raised and, of course, the total size of the crop at harvesttime. Whatever else it might be, life in China is not free from taxes. Each production brigade in a commune pays around 5 to 6 percent of its income in taxes to the government. An equal portion goes to a welfare fund for health and old age care. From 5 to 10 percent is deducted to purchase farm machinery. The remainder is distributed among members of the brigade. In the Red Star Commune near Peking, for example, income per head rose from 180 renminpi in 1958 to 330 renminpi in 1967. At the Valley of Stones Brigade in Hopei province, on the other hand, income per head fell from 131 renminpi in 1958 to 120 renminpi in 1967. At the Clay Hill Commune, also near Peking, per household income reportedly went from 400 renminpi in 1958 to 600 renminpi ten years later. In Fashih Commune in Kwangtung province, one household of five working adults in 1967 reportedly received 2,000 renminpi income, 200 of that from the sale of pigs and chickens members raised independently and for themselves.

In agriculture as in industry China still has a long way to go. The nation, from time to time, has had to purchase grain from abroad. And within the government there has been controversy over the question of whether to loosen reins and allow more individual production and personal gain. There has also been controversy at the other extreme, over some officials' belief that common peasant ownership of land, machinery, and factories should be abolished and all private plots be eliminated as well. These officials wish to gear production exclusively to the state, not to individual benefit at all.

The commune system has served as a device to relate urban and rural life, to try to increase production, and, of particular importance, to instill Communist attitudes and conduct among country people. The system might undergo alteration. But most observers do not think it will be abolished in the foreseeable future.

Training to become a doctor, a young woman practices the technique of acupuncture.

As the new regime took power in 1949, Mao Tse-tung as its chairman and as chairman of the Chinese Communist Party described the government as a democratic coalition under Communist Party leadership and a dictatorship aimed against reactionary classes and other "enemies of the people" such as landlords. The new administration took office with Chou En-lai as prime minister. Various aspects of the government were tied together by Communist leadership in the Central Committee, as the Party itself grew in membership from 2.7 million in 1947 to over 17 million in the 1960s. "To become a Party member," a factory worker told some visitors to China,

you submit an application; you should also be recommended by two members of the Party. Then a process of discussion follows, both within the Party and among the people you work with. These discussions sometimes stretch over a long period of time. Tsun Chiu-lan, a young woman worker at the Shenyang Transformer Factory, told us she first applied to join the Party in 1966. After she applied Party members "paid more attention to my growth and education," and "gave me help and education, so my consciousness was raised." She was approved

for membership in 1969. Both Party members and workers who are not in the Party discuss an applicant and whether they are qualified for Party membership. The final decision, however, is made by the local Party branch or group. Party members are generally the most active and politically advanced section of workers in a factory. Party members will often be responsible for leading study groups and are expected to take the lead in working on technical innovations and political struggle.

Under the Chinese constitution, China is governed by groups called congresses. On the village level, the people vote to elect representatives to local congresses, and everyone eighteen years old has the right to cast a ballot. A group of villages forms a county. Village congresses elect representatives to the county governments. County congresses, in turn, send representatives to provincial governments. There members of congresses elect representatives to the National Congress.

The National Congress is responsible for making laws for all China. In practice, however, this body's main activity is to approve laws and actions recommended by the Communist Party. Actual power is exercised through the Political Bureau of nineteen mem-

Opposite: The signboard under which this man stands, with its heroic figures steeled for action, is a typical Chinese movie advertisement. Most movies are designed to arouse patriotic feelings.

bers and the Bureau's Standing Committee of seven persons. Below this Bureau are 6 regional bureaus, 28 city or provincial committees, 258 special district committees, 2,200 county committees, and about 26,000 local committees. Finally, there are some 1 million branch committees in factories, villages, schools, and in the army.

Mass organizations with millions of members each, such as the All China Federation of Trade Unions, Democratic Youth, and Young Pioneers, help bridge the gap between officialdom and the people. These organizations can be relied on to help maintain socialist thinking among the people and to create and maintain popular support for government policies.

THOUGHT REFORM

In the beginning and periodically since then, the government conducted "thought reform" campaigns. Broadly speaking, thought reform meant complete control of a person's environment and of the information available to him. It included a mixture of idealistic and terror-producing stimuli. Guidance was always at hand to steer a person toward the required goal and, when necessary, develop in him a sense of guilt or shame for past misconduct or wrong thoughts. In many instances, people were forced to write and then rewrite confessions of guilt. Thought reform was carried out on a particularly large scale in new revolutionary colleges erected by the government and this, generally speaking, is how it operated:

A center of this type containing about four thousand students might be subdivided into classes of one or two hundred and then into study groups of six to ten persons. A typical six-month course of thought reform might consist of three stages. First, group identi-

fication, a period of togetherness and considerable freedom and enthusiasm. During this stage major Marxist-Leninist-Maoist concepts were studied and a free exchange of views, with a feeling of common effort, led the trainee to expose himself freely in a "thought mobilization."

The second phase was one of induced emotional conflict within each individual. The daily schedule continued to be physically exhausting. The environment, carefully controlled behind the scenes, now seemed to close in. The individual began to feel under pressure as criticism and self-criticism intensified and the dangers of being rejected became apparent. The evils within the old individual were now attacked, not merely the old society in the abstract, and the student strove to dig up his failings and correct them. He might struggle with himself and be "struggled with" by his groupmates over an excess of subjectivism or objectivism, of opportunism or dogmatism, of bureaucratism or individual heroism, and so forth. Each participant, whether or not he resisted, felt completely alone. He soon felt guilt (he should be punished) and also a sense of shame. He was thus prepared to achieve a psychological release through confession and self-condemnation.

The third phase was that of submission and rebirth. When his final thought summary or confession had been gone over and accepted, the individual was likely to feel exhilarated, cleansed, a new person. He had been manipulated so that the wellsprings of his own nature had put him under intense emotional pressure, and the relief from this self-induced tension was associated with the external authority of the party, on which he should henceforth be dependent. The party's aim was not only to secure control over disciplined activists but also to raise the quality of their performance by changing their goals and values. They renounced family and father, and accepted the party and the revolution in their place.

THE LOCAL LEVEL

On the village level the structure of government remains much the same as it always has been. There are still village heads and vice-heads, no longer selected by the gentry, but by higher governmental levels. They are generally appointed on the recommendation of Communist cadres within the villages on the basis of apparent leadership and popular qualities. Frequently village heads might be young men in their twenties, a broad departure from a past that placed top value on age and the wisdom it supposedly carried. Although structure remains about the same, the function of village government has increased considerably. Previously village governments were largely concerned with tax collection and with the enforcement and execution of orders handed down from above. Village governments still are. But in addition they are also concerned with schools, individual and family welfare, the performance of agricultural tasks, even with the orientation of a person's thought.

The local autonomy that once existed in the village is no more. Through the Communist Party and formal governmental relationships, villages are firmly tied to higher levels and finally to the national government. Government policy is constantly elaborated on and explained to the people through mass meetings, small group discussions, newspaper reading groups, and through political posters and news and information bulletins posted on the walls of public buildings. Formerly, only well-educated Chinese were likely to discuss public affairs. Peasants now are required to listen to such discussions and to participate in them as well. Discussion meetings serve as an additional means for the government to explain and defend policies and to protect and maintain the changes it has made in China. To what extent such events alter peasant thoughts and attitudes, of course, is anybody's guess. At any rate, the Chinese peasant appears to be more involved in affairs outside the village than he ever was before, whether that be to his benefit or not.

THE INDIVIDUAL AND THE LAW

There exist both criminal and civil law in China, but, many visitors insist, on the whole there is relatively little crime. Here again, reliable statistics are hard to come by, so it remains difficult to compare past with present, or China with any other country in this respect. Some visitors vowed that not only is the crime rate low, but even things lost or left in hotel rooms are preserved and faithfully returned to their owners. Whether such cases are common or exceptional, no one can say.

Visitors have frequently remarked on the cleanliness of Chinese city streets, at least the most prominent ones. They find no strong evidence of a drug problem, and little juvenile delinquency. Chinese youth the world around has long been noted for its tendency to stay out of trouble with authorities. The main reasons for this, apparently, are strong traditional family bonds and the persistence of filial piety. Even though the Chinese government has sought to shift loyalty from family to state, it would appear that the family remains a strong institution in China. Still, considering that country's vast size and population, it would hardly be surprising to learn that some people—both young and old—find themselves in trouble with the law now and then.

In the early 1960s it was reported that there were only three thousand lawyers in all of China, among a population then numbering something over 700 million. An important reason for this small number is the Chinese court system and its method of administration. As under French law, in China an accused person is presumed guilty until proved innocent. If police find a case against a person, the procurator—prosecuting attorney for whatever level of government it is—draws up an indictment. He then holds an examination. The majority of minor cases are decided at that level. If the person maintains innocence or the crime is major, like theft, a trial is held before a judge. Juries are not used in China. If the person chooses, he may have a lawyer defend him at five renminpi per day, which the court pays if the defendant cannot. There no longer is punishment or absence of it owing to class in China today, but judges enjoy great leeway in sentencing between a minimum and a maximum, and a convicted person may appeal the verdict to the next highest level. Few verdicts are appealed and even fewer reversed.

A person may be sentenced to from one to three years imprisonment in a city jail, from three to five years or longer at work on a state reform farm, or to restricted freedom or work under surveillance for a year or less. Counterrevolutionary activity, murder, and assault with intent to kill are capital crimes. So is rape of a victim under fourteen years of age. Upon conviction for any one of these, a person may be sentenced to death. Even under these circumstances, however, a person might be sentenced to two years in prison and rehabilitation attempted. If it proves successful, the person might receive only a light additional sentence.

As journalist Edgar Snow notes, reform, rehabilitation, and education have been traditional in Chinese thought. Confucians believed that those who knew the difference between good and evil possessed the duty of teaching others by word and by example. Mao Tse-tung, like Confucius and his followers, as he indicated on numerous occasions, believed that man could be perfected by education.

This, of course, does not make China unique. Personal change and betterment through education have long been an article of faith in western societies. And the idea remains very much alive today, in the United States and elsewhere. It is interesting to observe that in China, where much has changed in society, an age-old idea persists and gives no indication of diminishing or dying out, even though leaders have gone out of their way to try to dampen other aspects of Confucianism.

A DAY IN COURT

Snow was permitted to witness a court case in Shanghai, that of a prisoner named Yang Kuan-fu before a young judge, Mo Pen-wan. The charge was embezzlement of 1,527 renminpi by falsifying reports while Yang was a bill collector with the light and power company. It was brought under Section Three of the Criminal Code.

Yang Kuan-fu had been a policeman under Chiang Kai-shek's regime engaged in political and intelligence work. He admitted that he "arrested and tortured people to extract money from them, part of which I kept for myself. I helped carry out some looting also. With others, I took part in a few highway robberies." This, however, had nothing to do with the current charge under which Yang had been arrested on September 14, 1960, although the confession certainly did not help him.

Several witnesses, some of them accountants with the light and power company, testified against Yang. Then,

When the defendant had admitted to all the accusations, the judge asked him whether he realized that he had been robbing the working people and his own family, and whether he realized the seriousness of his crime. He said that he did, and added: "While the whole country is going forward I have been leaping backward. The government had given me a new way of life despite my corrupt past life. I was not satisfied with ample wages. I was greedy and wanted more."

The prosecutor then demanded maximum punishment in accordance with the law. The accused had not voluntarily confessed his crimes. Even after his fellow workers had discovered the first instance of embezzlement, the previous May, he had refused to help them by admitting his other crimes. Only after they had gathered all the evidence and had him arrested had he confessed to the police.

Judge Mo next heard from the defense attorney, who spoke in the following sense: "The accused has confessed and expressed his regret. Article Three is two-sided. It provides for punishment but also for reform through education. With us it is a principle to be lenient to those who repent and to be severe with those who do not. After his arrest the accused did quickly confess, and confess thoroughly. After a trip in the countryside he himself has seen how everyone is working to build the country up while he was tearing it down. This is true even in his own family. Now he feels ashamed. We should consider the corrupt life he formerly lived and make allowances. I consider his attitude relatively good. I would recommend leniency."

Judge Mo turned to the prisoner, who was visibly shaking. "Have you anything to say?" Yang replied in a quavering voice with one sentence only: "I shall do my best to carry out whatever punishment is given to me and to reform myself into a morally fit citizen."

Yang Kuan-fu could have received ten years' imprisonment for his crime. The judge sentenced him to three. "The crime was serious but the prisoner has now fully confessed and seems ready to rehabilitate himself," the judge said. "We consider that after some re-education he can still do something useful in society."

A sentry guards the People's Palace in Peking, seat of China's National Assembly.

THE DYNASTIC CYCLE

Change came to China without much help from the outside world. Relations with the Soviet Union after the Communist victory in China were friendly. Both are huge nations, both Communist. Their histories, however, were much different and, as a consequence, so were their styles of Communism. Russian Communist leaders had based their revolution on the proletariat—urban workers—while Mao had tied his revolution and his victory to the peasantry. Having brought about the first Communist revolution, and heading a vast and powerful nation, Soviet leaders considered themselves the chief guides and directors of Communism throughout the world. Theirs was the pure Communism. Mao and other Chinese leaders disagreed, not wishing to follow the Soviet lead and example.

The Soviet Union sent many advisors to China during the 1950s. Russia supplied money and equipment to help China build. But as the ideological split widened, relations between the two nations cooled. In the early 1960s the Chinese sent all Russian advisors home.

Russia and China share a long common border in Asia. On both sides the border remains heavily garrisoned. There have been numerous border clashes and threats of war.

Peace between the Communist giants remains uneasy.

For many years the United States government remained bitterly opposed to Communism regardless of the country in which it was found. Officially the United States government would have nothing to do with Mao's government. It insisted that Chiang Kai-shek's regime on Taiwan was the only legal Chinese government.

Unfriendly relations between China and the United States led to undeclared warfare between American and Chinese troops in Korea in 1951. Following World War II, Korea was split along the thirty-eighth parallel between North Korea, under a Communist government, and South Korea, under a government supported by the United States. In June 1950 North Korea invaded the south. North Korean leaders insisted that the government of South Korea, which had been defeated in elections but still held power, was no longer legal. The United States, along with some other nations of the United Nations, dispatched troops to aid South Korea. United Nations troops, composed largely of Americans, quickly pushed Communist troops back into North Korea. United Nations pursuit continued. But as those troops neared the Yalu River, which separates Korea from China, the Chinese government,

Opposite: Schoolchildren loose thousands of balloons as part of Peking's annual May Day celebration.

without warning, launched an attack on United Nations troops. Chinese attacks were successful, the Chinese driving United Nations forces back to the thirty-eighth parallel. There, after many months of bickering and negotiation, the Korean War ended.

China's foreign relations were unsettled, and within the country Mao's regime experienced numerous ups and downs. There were periods of severe internal strife and turmoil.

Believing that some intellectuals—professors, technicians, writers and others—had been won over to socialism, government leaders decided in 1956 to loosen strict control and stimulate intellectual life. That spring Mao announced, "Let a hundred flowers bloom, and a hundred schools of thought contend," referring back to Confucian times in China, when the Hundred Schools of philosophy had prevailed. Mao asked educated people to offer suggestions and criticisms concerning life under Communism.

Mao had expected criticism to remain within bounds, to proceed along accepted channels. He got much more than he bargained for. Criticism was tremendous, threatening soon to undermine the Communist regime and to drive China once again into turbulence. The Hundred Flowers soon wilted. Mao turned the criticism off.

THE GREAT LEAP FORWARD

Then, in the fall of 1957, Mao Tse-tung launched the Great Leap Forward. Under this plan China would do two things at once. It would greatly and quickly increase food production. It would at the same time greatly and quickly boost the production of tractors, machines, and other industrial products.

Cadres fanned out into the countryside to urge and inspire the people to produce more.

Peasants were admonished to work even longer hours and take no days off. Thousands of small furnaces for producing iron were set up in villages—"backyard factories"—to supply iron to large iron and steel industries. Workers in factories themselves were, like peasants, urged to put in longer hours and produce greater quantities of goods.

During the Great Leap Forward thousands of reservoirs and electrical power plants were constructed. Hundreds of miles of new highways and railroads were laid. Bridges and new canals were built. But by 1958 the Great Leap had collapsed from the people's sheer exhaustion. The plan had proved much too ambitious. No nation, especially a poor one like China, could hope to increase both farm and industrial production on such a vast scale in such a short time. China had insufficient trained manpower to meet the goals that had been set, and peasants and factory labor alike grew tired of being pushed to work harder and harder. Production increased, but only a little and only in certain areas. Food production did not keep up with the increase in population, and the early 1960s were poor crop years in China. As a result the government had to buy grain from Canada and Australia. China experienced a few years of economic dislocation and agricultural and industrial stagnation following the failure of the Great Leap Forward.

CULTURAL REVOLUTION

The Great Leap troubled Mao, for he was blamed for its conception and its failure. His opponents in the government forced his resignation as chairman of the People's Republic, although he remained chairman of the Party.

Mao Tse-tung had yet another concern. The revolution had progressed for a number of years and a great deal had been accomplished. Still, there was much to be done before China would be a strong nation. And it seemed to Mao that the people were beginning to lose their revolutionary spirit. They seemed to be relaxing, tending to concentrate on private goals and comforts, overlooking the good of society as a whole. In addition, it seemed to Mao, the thousands of officials needed to run the government had turned inward too. Having a job and keeping it appeared more important to them than serving the people.

At the same time, the experts—scientists and technicians needed to modernize China—seemed to be developing into a separate and special class, an elite. It appeared to Mao that they were losing their "redness"—their zeal for Communism, reform, and service to the people—and emphasizing their "expertness"—the special skills and knowledge that set them apart from the people.

Mao saw cadres as a means of serving and stirring up the people. Others in the government viewed them as a means of achieving party unity and were willing to train them as a new elite to guide change within China. Mao favored decentralized control, more local decision-making and direction. Others sought to increase control and guidance from the top. And within the government, the controversy came down, finally, to red versus expert, the politically well-indoctrinated against the professionally trained person.

As a consequence, in 1966 Mao launched the Great Proletarian Cultural Revolution. It ran roughly from May 1966 to April 1968. And it kept China in turmoil during all those years.

Mao urged the people to "make their own revolution," and campaign against the "Four Olds"—old thoughts, old culture, old customs, and old habits. Except for primary schools, all schools in China were closed and youth formed into units called Red Guards, sporting green uniforms, five-cornered military caps, and sneakers. The Red Guards were to move out all over China and attack all old ways of

thinking and behaving, spreading the thoughts of Mao Tse-tung and reawakening the people. "Dare to be violent," Mao told the Red Guards. "To rebel is good." To counter opposition within the government and the party, Mao reached outside it for support, and he enjoyed the backing of the army as well. The great movement was really launched in the fall of 1966—although much action took place before that—when some eleven million youths gathered in mass rallies in Peking. Following speeches, they dispersed into the countryside to bring reform and abolish the Four Olds.

Violent the Red Guards were. Rebel they did, against everything that was old. And this included everyone older than themselves.

Red Guards attacked teachers, held them prisoner, and forced them to confess that they had been teaching wrong thoughts and ideas. One former Red Guard later described action in his middle school:

The work team left so that the students could "launch revolution by themselves." At 9 A.M. on June 12 the team handed over a blacklist to the preparatory revolutionary committee and made public the files of one teacher after another. One was accused of having been a member of the Kuomintang, the Nationalist Party; another was linked to the Nationalist Youth Corps during World War II. "Now it is in front of you," the work team said. "Let's see what stand you take." The students were now ready to use force in a "life-and-death class struggle" against the teachers, their class enemies.

But I did not know it would come so soon. At twelve o'clock on the same day, as a few of us were on our way back from a swim in the sea, we heard screams and shouts as we approached the school gate. Some schoolmates ran up to us shouting, "The struggle has begun! The struggle has begun!" I ran inside. On the athletic field and farther inside, before a new four-story classroom building, I saw rows of teachers, about forty or fifty in all, with black ink poured over their heads and faces so that they were now in reality a "black gang." Hanging on their necks were placards with such words as "reactionary academic authority So-and-So," "class enemy So-and-So," "capitalist roader So-and-So," "corrupt ringleader So-and-So," all epithets taken from the newspapers. On each placard was a red cross, making the teachers look like condemned prisoners awaiting execution. They all wore dunce caps painted with similar epithets and carried dirty brooms, shoes, and dusters on their backs. Hanging from their necks were pails filled with rocks. I saw the principal; the pail around his neck was so heavy that the wire had cut deep into his neck and he was staggering. All were barefoot, hitting broken gongs or pots as they walked around the field, crying out, "I am black gangster So-and-So." Finally, they all knelt down, burned incense and begged Mao Tse-tung to "pardon their crimes."

Red Guards charged into factories and harassed workers. They seized Communist Party leaders in cities and paraded them through the streets in dunce caps. They destroyed property. Wrote the same Red Guard who described the incident in the school:

Once I wanted the feeling of smashing to pieces with my own hands the expensive windshield of a car that belonged to the Municipal Party Committee. I picked up a heavy wooden stake and struck the windshield with all my strength. Kwang! Gone were several hundred dollars in one stroke! The driver was heartbroken; he criticized me for being unreasonable and not protecting the people's property. In reply, I patted the Mao quotation book in my breast pocket and said, "Chairman Mao has taught me 'Rebellion is justified.' Go reason with Chairman Mao, if you want!"

"Rebellion is justified" was our supreme guiding principle and most potent weapon in dealing with our detractors or opponents. Sometimes when people criticized our excesses, all we had to do was raise the Mao quotation plaque in front of them and say, "Open your eyes and take a hard look at what Chairman Mao teaches us to do!" Destroying pianos, smashing glass with fists, throwing knives into doors, damaging all sorts of equipment in the school—all was done in the name of "Rebellion is justified."

Ranging the countryside, Red Guards interrupted farm work, consumed food supplies, and in numerous instances terrorized peasants. Sometimes Red Guards fought pitched battles with their elders and in some cases the People's Liberation Army had to be called out to put down serious trouble. People were killed during the months the Red Guards ran freely in China. How many no one knows.

In December 1966 Mao Tse-tung decided that the Red Guards' work was completed. They were ordered to return home. But Chinese youth had found rebellion too good. The Red Guards refused. Turmoil and disorder continued.

Meanwhile, Mao moved against men in the government and in the Communist Party he considered threats to him. Many high officials were replaced. The Party was reorganized. In the provinces, hundreds of officials lost their jobs, replaced by persons deemed more truly in line with Mao's thoughts, ideas, and aims for China.

The Great Cultural Revolution gradually wound down. Toward the end of 1967 Mao announced that it had been a great success. The Four Olds had been eliminated. So had enemies of the people and of the Chinese Revolution. It was now time to return to the task of building China. "Revolutionaries must never act according to their own sweet will," said an official government newspaper.

This was a clear signal that the Great Cultural Revolution was at an end. People were now to go back to work. Still, many Red Guards did not take the hint. Schools were reopened, but thousands of youths refused to return to classes. As a consequence they were sent to work in factories, in mines, and on farms. Never again would they go to school.

CHINA AND OTHER NATIONS

Following the Cultural Revolution, China's relations with other nations began to change somewhat. The United States had been fighting a long war against Communist North Vietnam, which borders China. The possibility had existed that China and the United States might once again become involved in war. But in the late 1960s the United States began to wind down its war effort in Vietnam, owing largely to intense opposition to the war among Americans. Relations between the United States and China slowly began to improve. It is possible that this was due mainly to Chinese leaders' desire to counter-balance what they considered an ever-present threat from Soviet Russia.

In 1971, China replaced the Taiwan government as a member of the United Nations. In the meantime, American President Richard M. Nixon's chief foreign policy advisor, Henry Kissinger, conducted secret negotiations with the Chinese government. Then, early in 1972, President Nixon flew to China to confer with Mao, Chou En-lai, and other government leaders. This amounted to recognition that Communism had come to stay in China. It also indicated a direct 180-degree turn in United States policy toward China. Ambassadors were not immediately exchanged, but representatives almost on that

level were. United States-China trade reopened once again, after having been closed for many years. China began to receive visitors of numerous kinds from the United States, and a host of articles and books about China spewed forth from American presses. Americans could now obtain considerable information on which to base their understanding of China and changes which had occurred there.

Chinese Communist leaders see three things as outstanding in their country's history: feudalism as represented largely by the gentry, imperialism represented mainly by European nations and the Japanese, and a Kuomintang government which they insist was corrupt and oppressive. All three have been eliminated from Chinese life. Believing as they do, Communists prefer to speak of "Liberation" rather than of "Communist take-over."

Further, contrary to revolutions in such countries as the Soviet Union, the Chinese revolution was based on the peasantry. And government leaders appear to have kept in mind that the easiest way to create trouble for themselves is to get on the wrong side of the peasantry. Regardless of industrialization, the peasants must be kept satisfied or difficulties will ensue. They number in the hundreds of millions. Any Chinese government would therefore have to reckon with them.

THE FUTURE

Over the past century and more, the Chinese people have suffered much, to some extent because of their country's lack of industrial power. The Chinese were unable to resist European domination which began in the middle of the nineteenth century. They were unable to prevent the Japanese from moving in later, and then they underwent Japanese invasion. Right now China is moving along the path toward industrialization, and it appears that the country will maintain itself as the oldest and longest continuous civilization the world has ever known.

Undergoing its own industrial revolution, China has experienced mistakes, hardship, and some suffering. In this respect it is not unique. Other nations have had similar problems, for no one can foresee all the consequences of actions involved in establishing and expanding industry. Industrialization in England, where in the eighteenth century the Industrial Revolution began, brought low wages and poor working conditions for laborers, dreadful slums, and polluted cities. These consequences were gradually overcome, but the process required some time.

There is a school of thought which holds that as societies industrialize, they tend to resemble one another more and more. All take on the same values. Under the impact of industrialization, differences that mark cultures off from one another tend to diminish, even disappear. That is one viewpoint.

Another point of view holds that despite industrialization, cultures tend to remain different. Tradition and modernization are not mutually exclusive. Industrialized societies retain many aspects of tradition, cultures their own unique characteristics. According to this viewpoint, history is so influential that, despite the fact that similarities will be noticeable, no amount of industrialization will steamroller cultures into the same mold.

The Chinese experience might inspire a third school of thought. Traditionally China has had autocratic government. Traditionally the Chinese have been directed from the top. Traditionally government has been remote from the ordinary experience of the ordinary person. And, traditionally, Confucian principles on the whole governed behavior. China still has an autocratic government, although there are more means now by which citizens can make their needs known and receive responses. The Chinese are still directed from the top, but there is a good deal more local participation

and decision making than before. Government is no longer entirely separate from the people. And Confucian principles and their influence are not as strong as they used to be. Mao's Communists have made extensive changes, not only on the face of China, but also in the ways people think and regard each other and their society.

China will become a modern, industrial nation. But it would appear unlikely that it will become a "westernized" nation. It would also seem unlikely that industrialization will proceed, in the foreseeable future at least, under any but a socialistic system of the Chinese brand. There is little likelihood that China will return to the old way of life, although some tradition might be reinstated should the Chinese reach a point at which they can relax a little. Assuming socialism continues, even with industrialization China might well develop an enduring culture unlike any in the world, just as traditional Chinese civilization was unique.

Looking far down the road of history to imagine scenes not yet enacted, one might, like some scholars, at the same time glance back. There appears to have been a "dynastic cycle" in China that applied to all dynasties, at least from Shang to Ch'ing. The restoration of order, enthusiasm, change for the better, great public support, all marked the beginning of each dynasty. Strong, determined, and farsighted men ruled China. As good government reigned, Chinese culture flowered. Then, inevitably it seemed, came a downturn. Later rulers were not so determined, so powerful, so conscious of the necessity to tend to people's needs. Many were weak, immoral persons. The government proved unable to cope with national calamity, natural disasters such as floods, or invasion from without. The people suffered. Finally the Mandate of Heaven was withdrawn. A new dynasty won power.

Some dynasties were short, like the Ch'in, even though vitally influential. Others like the

Han, lasting four hundred years, and the Sung, enduring better than three hundred, seemed eternal. Even the Ch'ing, a foreign dynasty and the final one, lasted almost as long.

Do Communists in China constitute a new dynasty, taking power after many years of strife and turmoil? Will their reign be short, somewhat like the Ch'in, or much longer, like the Han? Will the Communist regime repeat the dynastic cycle? These are questions only time can answer, but for the student of more than four millennia of Chinese history they hold a certain fascination.

Many men made the Chinese revolution. Among them, Chou En-lai, as premier, served as an important stabilizing influence in the government which was established. Most observers agree, however, that the major responsibility for the changes which have taken place in China rest with the Communist long-time leader, Mao Tse-tung. It was he who continued to insist that peasants could be instruments of change, even during the years in the north in Shenshi province. And the fact that the Chinese revolution was peasant based is, perhaps, its most important characteristic.

A caretaker on the road to the Ming Tombs, north of Peking.

MAJOR CHINESE DYNASTIES

TO 1500 B.C.   **LEGENDARY RULERS**

1500–1027 B.C.   **SHANG DYNASTY**
Known principally through archeological findings

1027–256 B.C.   **CHOU DYNASTY**
Period of warring states
Time of Confucius

221–206 B.C.   **CH'IN DYNASTY**
First strong central government established
Name China derived
Great Wall built

206 B.C.–A.D. 220   **HAN DYNASTY**
Confucian bureaucracy established
Extension of China's borders
Paper invented

220–590   **PERIOD OF CHAOS AND WARRING STATES**
Beginning of Buddhism in China

590–618   **SUI DYNASTY**
Central government reestablished
Expansion into Korea fails

618–906   **T'ANG DYNASTY**
Printing invented
Great cultural flourishing

960–1279   **SUNG DYNASTY**
Gunpowder
Magnetic Compass
Moveable type

1279–1368   **YÜAN (MONGOL) DYNASTY**
Many visitors such as Marco Polo from the West
Increased trade between China and the West

1368–1644	**MING DYNASTY** Contacts with West halted China secluded
1644–1911	**CH'ING (MANCHURIAN) DYNASTY** West "reopens" China Period of unequal treaties Manchus toppled by 1911 Revolution
1912	**REPUBLIC OF CHINA ESTABLISHED**
1949	**COMMUNIST GOVERNMENT UNDER MAO TSE-TUNG ESTABLISHED**

Emperor Wu-ti and his attendants, painted by Yen Li-pen, a court artist of the T'ang Dynasty.

INDEX

ACKNOWLEDGMENTS

Columbia University Press: For material from *A Chinese Village* by Martin C. Yang; copyright 1945 by Columbia University Press. Crown Publishers, Inc.: For material from *Chinese Fairy Tales* by Isabell C. Chang; copyright © 1965 by Barre Publishers. Doubleday & Company, Inc.: For material from *Americans and Chinese* by Francis L. K. Hsu; copyright © 1953, 1970 by Francis L. K. Hsu. Eastern Horizon: For "Women in China" by Julian Schuman, "Education in China and China in Education" by Ronald Frankenberg, "Agriculture and Industry in Two Chinese Hinterland Counties" by Rewi Alley, and "Chinese Factories" by Goldwasser and Dowty. Houghton Mifflin Company: For material from *East Asia: Tradition and Transformation* by Fairbank, Reischauer and Craig; copyright © 1973 by Houghton Mifflin Company. Little, Brown and Company: For material from *800,000,000: The Real China* by Ross Terrill; copyright © 1971, 1972 by Ross Terrill. Monthly Review Press: For material from *Fanshen* by William Hinton; copyright © 1966 by William Hinton. Oxford University Press: For material from *Modern Chinese Stories,* selected and edited by W. J. F. Jenner. Pergamon Press Ltd.: For material from *Society, Schools, and Progress in China* by Tsang Chiu-sam; copyright 1968 by Pergamon Press. Praeger Publishers, Inc.: For material from *Birth of Communist China* by C. P. Fitzgerald; copyright 1966 by Praeger Publishers, Inc. G. P. Putnam's Sons: For material from *The Revenge of Heaven* by Ken Ling; copyright © 1972 by Dr. Ivan London and Miriam London. Random House, Inc.: For material from *The China Reader: People's China*, edited by David Milton, Nancy Milton and Franz Schurmann; copyright © 1974 by David Milton, Nancy Milton and Franz Schurmann. For material from *The Other Side of the River* by Edgar Snow; copyright © 1961, 1962 by Edgar Snow. For material from *Report from a Chinese Village* by Jan Myrdal, translated by Maurice Michael; copyright © 1965 by William Heinemann Ltd., reprinted by permission of Pantheon Books, a division of Random House, Inc. For material from *The Wisdom of China and India*, edited and translated by Lin Yutang; copyright 1942 and renewed 1970 by Random House, Inc. St. Martin's Press: For material from *A Short History of China* by Hilda Hookham; copyright 1970 by St. Martin's Press.

ILLUSTRATIONS

Christina Gascoigne, cover, 20, 34; Der Stern, Black Star, 2, 110; Collection C. A. Drenowatz, Zürich, on loan at Rietberg Museum, Zürich, 8; Dmitri Kessel, Courtesy of The People's Republic of China, 10; Eugene Fuller Memorial Collection, Seattle Art Museum, 17; William Rockhill Nelson Gallery of Art, 25, 57; Joan Lebold Cohen, 26; Los Angeles County Museum of Art, The Ernest Larsen Blanck Memorial Fund, 28; Courtesy of John Weatherhill Inc., 40, 41; Courtesy, Museum of Fine Arts, Boston, 46, 139; Honolulu Academy of Arts, 48; The Metropolitan Museum of Art, 54, 58; The Cleveland Museum of Art, Bequest of John L. Severance, 60; Courtesy of The Brooklyn Museum, gift of Samuel P. Avery, 61; John Thomson, Courtesy of The Art Institute of Chicago, 66; Cecil Beaton, 68, 78; Henri Cartier-Bresson, Magnum, 73; James Burke, Graphic House, 86; Richard J. Balzer, 90, 93, 104, 137; René Burri, Magnum, 91, 135; Marc Riboud, Magnum, 92, 102, 122, 127, 136; from *China Pictorial*, Number 2, 1968, 94; Dmitri Kessel, Time-Life Picture Agency, © Time Inc., 95, 116; Audrey Topping, 96; Anglo-Chinese Educational Institute, 121; Brian Brake, Rapho/Photo Researchers, 128